Soviet Leaders and Intelligence

Soviet Leaders and Intelligence

Assessing the American Adversary during the Cold War

Raymond L. Garthoff

Georgetown University Press / Washington, DC

Library of Congress Cataloging-in-Publication Data

Garthoff, Raymond L., author.
    Soviet leaders and intelligence : assessing the American adversary during the Cold War / Raymond L. Garthoff.
       pages   cm
    Includes bibliographical references and index.
    Summary: The United States was seen by Soviet political leaders as the "Main Adversary" throughout the Cold War, and Soviet intelligence services were renowned and feared throughout the world for their ability to conduct espionage and dirty tricks. This work by Raymond Garthoff examines the Soviet foreign intelligence system broadly to evaluate how Soviet leaders and their intelligence chiefs understood, or misunderstood, the United States. This extended case study shows a paradox in the Soviet foreign intelligence system, that as good and feared as Soviet intelligence was at operations, their analysis of intelligence was mediocre and under-resourced. Furthermore, Soviet leaders were more frequently guided by their personal views and Party ideology than by intelligence. This work synthesizes new and old sources on Soviet intelligence and Soviet political leaders to give the most authoritative assessment to date of the Soviets' understanding of the United States. This work is an important case study for the history of intelligence analysis, and it is also an important corrective for those who see Soviet intelligence as an all-powerful and all-knowing force during the Cold War.
    ISBN 978-1-62616-229-7 (pb : alk. paper) — ISBN 978-1-62616-228-0 (hc : alk. paper) — ISBN 978-1-62616-230-3 (eb)
    1. Soviet Union—Foreign relations—United States. 2. United States—Foreign relations—Soviet Union. 3. Soviet Union—Foreign relations—1945–1991. 4. Intelligence service—Soviet Union. 5. Politicians—Soviet Union. I. Title.

E183.8.S65G385 2015
327.47073—dc23

                                   2014043611

♾ This book is printed on acid-free paper meeting the requirements of the American National Standard for Permanence in Paper for Printed Library Materials.

16 15   9 8 7 6 5 4 3 2 First printing

Printed in the United States of America

Cover design by Jim Keller. Cover image courtesy of the Library of Congress.

Contents

Preface   vii

Introduction   ix

Chronology of Key Events Affecting US-Soviet Relations,
  1945–91   xvii

ONE   Stalin: Emergence of the Cold War, 1945–53   1

TWO   Khrushchev: Thaw and Crisis, 1954–64   17

THREE   Brezhnev: Engagement and Détente, 1965–79   37

FOUR   Brezhnev, Andropov: Tensions Revived, 1979–84   57

FIVE   Gorbachev: Back to Détente—and Beyond,
            1985–91   74

Conclusions   95

Appendix 1: Soviet Leaders, 1945–91   103
Appendix 2: Heads of the Soviet State Security Organization,
  1945–91   104
Appendix 3: Heads of Soviet Foreign Intelligence, 1945–91   105
Appendix 4: US-Soviet Summit Meetings, 1945–91   106
Notes   107
Index   133

Preface

I was a close observer of Soviet policy throughout the Cold War, first at Princeton and Yale from 1945 to 1950, then as an analyst at the RAND Corporation and the Central Intelligence Agency throughout the 1950s and as a US Department of State officer and diplomat in the 1960s and 1970s. Since 1980 I have been a diplomatic historian of the Cold War as a senior fellow at the Brookings Institution and in retirement. During and after the Cold War, I have had considerable contact with Soviet officials, diplomats, intelligence officers, military leaders, and academic specialists. This has provided a background foundation for research and analysis based on Soviet and Western open and official (including declassified archival) publications, as well as interviews and less formal conversations with former "adversaries."

I would like to acknowledge the assistance of my brother Douglas in preparing this study. His wise counsel and careful review of multiple drafts helped to sharpen my thinking with respect to a number of points, and his constant support of the study and untiring attention to myriad practical tasks ensured its successful completion.

Introduction

The United States was seen by Soviet political leaders, and by their intelligence services, as the Soviet Union's "Main Adversary" (*glavnyi protivnik*) throughout the Cold War. In 1945–47, as the wartime alliance of the victors dissolved, the United States came to be so regarded in Moscow mainly owing to its unrivaled and newly confirmed predominance in the capitalist world system, the perception shaped by a combination of ideological determinism and geopolitical rivalry. Even as the Soviet Union's efforts to bolster its control in most of the areas it had occupied during the war led the West to see a threat from Soviet expansionism, Soviet leaders—above all Josef Stalin—saw a threat to the USSR's security from an American-led Western bloc waging political warfare against it. The United States had come, in their eyes, to earn the distinction of being their main adversary.

The nature of the Cold War confrontation and the perceptions and policies of the two sides evolved over time, ultimately ending not in Armageddon but in the collapse of the Soviet system. This book seeks to clarify that evolution from the perspective of the changing understanding of the American adversary that the USSR's political leaders and intelligence services derived from their ideology, foreign intelligence, and interactions with the West. It concludes that, overall, intelligence fared poorly in competition with other influences and sources of information and that, in the end, a bold decision by the USSR's last leader to alter fundamentally the Soviet conception of international politics ended America's status as the Soviet Union's main adversary.

Studies of intelligence and its role in supporting the top political leaders of nations often focus on the accuracy of the information and analysis supplied to the leaders by their intelligence services. This study seeks to illuminate a different dimension of the interaction between the political recipients of intelligence assessments and the intelligence chiefs who provide them, namely, how the perceptions and objectives of political leaders and their intelligence chiefs interacted, affecting both how intelligence assessments were shaped and how they were received.

The study of perceptions in international relations remains less well developed than deserved. Although excellent studies have been written by outstanding scholars such as historian Ernest May and political scientist Robert Jervis, the views of political leaders—encompassing in each case an admixture of subjective biases, assumptions, knowledge, and experience—and the impact of those views on national policies remains a rich field for further inquiry. This study seeks to contribute to this field by describing the nature and sources of the leadership perceptions of one of the two main adversaries of the Cold War.

The book is organized chronologically. After describing the setting for the Cold War, it takes up Stalin's views and those of Soviet intelligence officers and diplomats as they defined their main adversary during a period of intensifying confrontation in the wake of World War II. It then describes changes brought after Stalin's death in 1953 by Nikita Khrushchev and other leaders, who gradually added lessons learned from interacting with Americans to views still heavily influenced by ideology as they began to revise Soviet policy toward the West. The next chapter describes the shift by Leonid Brezhnev and his colleagues after Khrushchev's ouster in 1964 from his bluster and risky moves to a more settled view of America as a kind of partner as well as rival and main adversary and the emergence of a postwar generation of diplomats, academics, and intelligence officers who deepened Soviet study of America and expanded interactions with American counterparts. The study then assesses the period from the mid-1970s to the mid-1980s when an aging Soviet leadership underwent successive changes and weathered renewed US-Soviet tensions related to global competition, an intensifying arms race, and harsh assessments by both sides of the other in the early 1980s. The chapter dealing with Mikhail Gorbachev's leadership beginning in 1985 shows how startling changes in Soviet thinking about world politics brought about unexpected Soviet policies and facilitated a surprisingly rapid and peaceful end of the Cold War. A concluding chapter presents observations and lessons about the changes in Soviet views of the United States during the remarkable forty-five-year period when the two adversaries waged a global political battle under the constant shadow of potential nuclear war.

The Cold War

Marxism-Leninism posited an ineluctable conflict between the capitalist (imperialist) world and an emerging socialist (communist) world. That ideological framework did not preclude Soviet leaders from acting according to the practices of the old world they saw as surrounding and threatening the USSR, but it did lead them to believe there was an objective and historically determined underlying adversarial relationship. Prior to World War II, Soviet leaders and intelligence officers considered Great Britain to be the USSR's main adversary in the international arena. The United States took on this role only after the war.

The conviction of successive Soviet leaders that they were on the right side of an inexorable revolutionary historical process engendered in Western leaders the counterconviction that they had no recourse but to accept the challenge of their self-declared adversary and engage in an imposed competition. There were unique features of the perceptions of each side, but most important was a feature common to both: a reciprocated image of the other side as an adversary and the attribution to it of hostile intent, fueling potential confrontation and a constant arms buildup. These views virtually ensured the outcome that ensued: the Cold War.

Some have argued that owing to these ideological precepts of Marxist-Leninist communism, postulating an inexorable revolutionary historical process of class-based conflict destined to override the traditional system of nation-states, the Cold War should be considered to have begun with the Bolshevik (communist) seizure of power in Russia in October 1917 and its inherent challenge to the existing world order.[1] The main seeds of the Cold War do, indeed, stem from that ideological conviction of successive leaders of the Communist Party of the Soviet Union—together with the counterconviction engendered in the Western powers that they had no recourse but to accept the challenge of their self-declared adversary and engage in the imposed confrontation. It is historically more accurate and useful, however, to consider the Cold War as having emerged over the years 1945 to 1950 under the impact of three interrelated contemporaneous developments in those years.

First came the utter defeat of the two most aggressive military great powers, Germany and Japan, and the need for the three principal victorious Allies (of convenience and necessity)—no longer bound by their common wartime goal—to reorder the shattered international system, above all its European center.

Second, the defeat and collapse of Germany, Japan, and Italy, the earlier defeat of France, and the wartime weakening of the former main adversary, Great Britain and its empire, left a unique bipolar rivalry of the two remaining great powers, the United States and the Soviet Union. The Soviet Union, to be sure, had also been weakened in many important ways by the tremendous losses of the war, but it retained substantial military power in occupation of nearly half of Europe. Nonetheless, from the perspective of its leaders, it was now no longer one of half a dozen great powers but one of three, and by 1947 one of but two, as well as unique as a communist state positioned soon to lead a group of new communist satellite states.

In the prewar 1920s and 1930s, the Soviet leaders had seen the USSR as a threatened socialist island surrounded by a hostile capitalist encirclement. The capitalist/imperialist powers were believed to be compulsive competitors for power among themselves, however, and the central task of Soviet diplomacy had been to discern and play upon imperialist rivalries in order to prevent a coalition of these powers from coalescing in alliance against the Soviet Union. Now, in the aftermath of a second world war, while the Soviet Union needed time and peace to build its strength, the capitalist world had also been weakened by the war and would soon be faced by the growing potential role of formerly weak members such as China, as well as the imperialist colonies of India and other countries of South and Southeast Asia, the Middle East, Africa, and Latin America. Those emerging countries were expected to enter a transition from dependencies of European states in the capitalist world to becoming "people's democracies" and eventually members of the new socialist camp headed by the Soviet Union. This view developed mainly with decolonization in the 1960s and 1970s, but as early as the late 1940s this process was seen as weakening the imperialist camp and as a further source of competition within it, as well as a source of eventual contribution to a growing socialist world. The victory of the communists in China in 1949 was seen as a major loss for the capitalist world and a harbinger of the future (although also as presenting some new problems for maintaining Soviet leadership of the new socialist camp). And it was anticipated that Germany and Japan would seek to regain great-power status and politico-military weight. But the dominating element in the near run was the emergence of a geopolitical bipolarity of the two superpowers as the United States succeeded Great Britain as the new preponderant and leading power of the old world facing the Soviet Union.

The third defining factor of the Cold War was the dawn of the nuclear age, with the United States dropping an atomic (nuclear) bomb on Hiroshima, Japan, in August 1945. The American decision during the war not to share its nuclear secrets, and after the war to offer a plan for international control (the Baruch Plan, in 1946) under which only the United States would have possessed the ability to produce nuclear weapons, reflected a lack of trust but was only what Stalin and his cohorts expected—and would have done had they been in the position to do so.

The United States in 1945 was the sole possessor of nuclear

weapons. But, as Soviet leader Stalin and his colleagues knew, this would not long remain the case. The Soviet Union, as well as the United States, had had a program under way during the war, and Soviet scientific skill was buttressed and the path to nuclear weapons facilitated by extensive successful Soviet espionage penetration of the American and British wartime nuclear weapons development programs. By 1947 Foreign Minister Vyacheslav Molotov could declare (without elaboration) that the Soviet Union too had the secret of the atomic bomb, and by August 1949 the Soviet Union had tested its first such weapon. Military power, and political power as well, in yet undefined ways was rapidly changing. Now, by the end of the decade, a new constellation of power distinguished the two nuclear superpowers from all others (including those that later also produced limited numbers of nuclear weapons) throughout the Cold War.

Some revisionist historians have posited a more direct and even primary role in unleashing the Cold War to the American use of the first atomic weapon against Japan in 1945, ascribing to US leaders the intention of displaying this terrible new weapon of mass destruction primarily not to win the war against Japan but as a demonstration of American power in a latent threat to the Soviet Union in a new contest for world domination.[2] Most important, and tending to refute that interpretation, was that Stalin evidently did not so regard the Hiroshima bombing.[3] He expected the United States to attempt to parlay this new powerful weapon into leverage on the Soviet Union, but he correctly believed it would not lead the United States to attack the Soviet Union or threaten its use by issuing ultimatums. Indeed, for more than a year after Hiroshima, Stalin believed it would still be possible to work out a Yalta-course collaborative arrangement with the United States and Great Britain. Moreover, the emergence of the Cold War over the late 1940s was at no point importantly affected by the US nuclear monopoly.

In 1945 it was still possible for the three victorious powers—the United States, the Soviet Union, and Great Britain—to work out a relationship that would serve their respective security needs and an international order. Some important steps were taken, notably the creation of the United Nations. But prospective geopolitical bipolarity in the nuclear age between one power that saw itself as historically destined to lead a revolutionary transformation of the entire international order, faced by another that would not accept that destiny and championed an alternative democratic capitalist world order, virtually ensured the Cold War.

Chronology of Key Events Affecting US-Soviet Relations, 1945–91

1945	February 4–11	Big Three leaders meet at Yalta
	April 13	Roosevelt dies
	May 8	World War II ends in Europe
	July 17–Aug. 2	Big Three leaders meet at Potsdam
	August 6	United States drops atomic bomb on Hiroshima
	September 2	World War II ends in Asia
1946	March 6	Churchill delivers "Iron Curtain" speech
1947	March 12	Truman Doctrine announced
	June 5	Marshall Plan announced
1948	June 24	Soviets begin blockade of West Berlin
1949	April 4	North Atlantic Treaty Organization (NATO) established
	August 28	Soviets conduct first atomic test
1950	April 14	NSC-68 sets out US containment policy
	June 25	North Korea invades South Korea
1953	March 5	Stalin dies
1955	May 14	Warsaw Pact signed
	July 18–23	Four Powers meet at Geneva
1958	November 10	Khrushchev initiates second Berlin Crisis
1960	May 1	US U-2 reconnaissance plane shot down over USSR
1962	October 22	Kennedy discloses Soviet missiles in Cuba
1964	August 7	Congress passes Tonkin Gulf (Vietnam) Resolution
1972	May 22	ABM Treaty, SALT I Agreement signed
1975	August 1	Helsinki (CSiCE) Accord on Europe signed
1979	December 27	Soviets invade Afghanistan
1983	September 1	Soviets shoot down KAL 007

1985	March 11	Gorbachev becomes top Soviet leader
1986	October 10	Gorbachev, Reagan meet at Reykjavik
1988	December 7	Gorbachev announces major unilateral arms cuts
1989	November 9	Berlin Wall begins to come down
	December 1	Gorbachev and Bush meet in Malta
1990	March 31	Warsaw Pact dissolved
	October 3	West Germany and East Germany unite
	November 26	Paris (CSCE) summit marks end of the Cold War
1991	August 19	Abortive coup launched in Moscow
	December 26	USSR dissolved

CHAPTER ONE

Stalin

Emergence of the Cold War, 1945–53

Although Josef Stalin, the leader since the late 1920s, always saw Western powers as adversaries, the crucible of war had forged Soviet collaboration with them even as they remained the objects of distrust. In the fall of 1943, Stalin established a commission headed by Deputy Foreign Affairs Commissar Maksim Litvinov to study issues concerning the postwar order. Former ambassador to London Ivan Maisky headed another commission on proposals for dealing with Germany and its allies. Litvinov and Maisky were the most "moderate" members of Stalin's entourage and probably the most knowledgeable of the West. Litvinov, who had an English wife and had served as Soviet representative in Britain and ambassador to the United States, had been foreign affairs commissar in the 1930s, and his replacement by Vyacheslav Molotov in May 1939 had signaled the end of Stalin's interest in a rapprochement with Britain and France and foreshadowed the signing of a Soviet-German treaty. Although Litvinov proposed a far-reaching "security perimeter" around the Soviet Union, the guidance under which the commissions operated assumed continuing cooperation with Great Britain and the United States after the war.[1]

Stalin did seek to continue the wartime Big Three partnership after the war, albeit in his own way. He envisaged a postwar great-power club of two or three equals with freedom to act within negotiated spheres of influence. He accepted the creation of the United Nations and other international organizations so long as he had a veto over any action that could impinge on his own sphere of influence or freedom of action. In 1945 the Big Three reached some major decisions on postwar arrangements at Yalta in February and Potsdam in July, and they took a number of practical measures that accommodated their interests.

In 1945–46 both sides did take a number of measures to meet earlier commitments. Liberated German-held prisoners of war were returned to their homelands (entailing a terrible fate for many Soviet POWs). The United States withdrew its forces from areas of eastern Germany assigned to the Soviet zone of occupation (and earlier had held back from occupying Prague and parts of eastern Germany). The Soviet Union, for its part, permitted American, British, and French forces into West Berlin and withdrew its own presence there and withdrew from areas it had occupied during the war in Denmark (Bornholm Island), northern Norway, and Bear Island. It also withdrew its forces from Manchuria in China. The United States and the Soviet Union agreed on withdrawal of their forces from Czechoslovakia, on rotating chairmanship of a joint occupation of Vienna with separate occupation sectors of Austria, and other mutual accommodations—albeit amid growing friction and failures at cooperation as time went on.

Although some major decisions on postwar cooperation had been made at Yalta and Potsdam, many issues remained, and new ones arose that proved contentious. Stalin sought, and was denied, occupation zones for the Soviet Union in northern Hokkaido and a role in the overall occupation in Japan and Italy. His only recourse was to deny the United States and Britain a role in the defeated minor Axis allies Hungary, Romania, and Bulgaria. Stalin also sought a military base in Danish Bornholm and economic rights in Spitsbergen. (He was in a position to retain a naval base in Finland and a base in Manchuria, both returned by his successor Nikita Khrushchev in 1955.) He sought, and was denied, the cession of the provinces of Kars and

Ardahan in northern Turkey (once Russian) and a major role in the Dardanelles Straits in Turkey. He even sought, and was denied, a UN trusteeship in former Italian-ruled Libya and Ethiopia in Africa. He delayed evacuation of Soviet troops from northern Iran in 1946 and left two nominally independent and separate new states there, but he did nothing to assist them when they were soon reoccupied by Iran. He had, of course, been able to use Soviet military occupation to establish satellite communist states in Eastern Europe—Poland, Romania, Hungary, Bulgaria, and East Germany.

Over time Stalin reluctantly concluded that he could not deal as successfully with Franklin D. Roosevelt's and Winston Churchill's successors as he had with them. Litvinov again became a bellwether of change in Soviet policy when his dismissal from the post of deputy foreign minister in late 1946 foreshadowed the end of Stalin's hopes of continuing a collaborative policy with the Western powers. However much Stalin valued Litvinov (whom he had first made commissar for foreign affairs in 1930), he clearly did not rely on his views in basic perceptions of, or formulating policies toward, the West.

Astonishingly frank criticisms of Stalin and his policies voiced by Litvinov to Westerners (of which Stalin was aware) revealed a side of Stalin's thinking that contributed to the increasingly adversarial nature of the postwar Soviet-American relationship. As early as May 1943, Litvinov had confessed to Undersecretary of State Sumner Welles that he was unable to communicate with Stalin, "whose isolation bred a distorted view of the West and especially an underestimation of Western public opinion." In an October 1944 conversation with the writer Edgar Snow, Litvinov implied that Stalin was prone to misconceptions, especially by reading too much into unfriendly statements in the free Western press. He also lamented that the Foreign Affairs Commissariat was run by three men (Molotov, Andrei Vyshinsky, and Vladimir Dekanozov), "and none of them understand America or Britain." A month later, in answering Ambassador Averell Harriman's query as to what the United States could do to satisfy the Soviet Union, he replied, "Nothing." Finally, in a June 1946 interview with American correspondent Richard Hottelet, Litvinov declared that the root cause of East-West tension was "the ideological conception prevailing here [in Moscow] that conflict between the communist and capitalist worlds is inevitable" and went on to state frankly that giving in to Soviet demands would only lead to new ones.[2]

Stalin's views of Western leaders combined suspicion of their connivance against him with hope that he could exploit divisions among them. Even at the height of Big Three wartime collaboration, Stalin had assumed that Churchill and Roosevelt would take any opportunity to weaken the Soviet Union. Soviet espionage kept Stalin well informed of Western positions at conferences and plans for opening a second front against Germany, and Stalin tasked it with keeping a sharp eye for signs of Western perfidy. Chief of foreign intelligence Gen. Pavel Fitin told Vasily Zarubin, the wartime chief of NKGB intelligence in the United States, that Stalin in 1941 had personally ordered him to pursue any leads indicating that Churchill and the Americans were seeking a separate peace with Germany or developing secret plans relating to postwar arrangements.[3] At the same time, Stalin had long believed that the United States would eventually challenge Great Britain for primacy in the capitalist world, and he was inclined during and immediately after the war to believe that British-American rivalry would provide opportunities for Soviet exploitation. Roosevelt, for reasons of his own, unknowingly buttressed this belief by seeking in Big Three wartime meetings to chide Churchill and persuade Stalin indirectly that there was no unified Anglo-American position.[4]

Soviet intelligence had multiple penetrations of the US and UK programs to develop the atomic bomb and other weapon-development projects, as well as the now well-known placements of Soviet agents in the diplomatic and intelligence services of the United Kingdom, including senior liaison officers in Washington Kim Philby (for the Secret Intelligence Service) and Donald Maclean (for the Foreign Office).[5] When Philby in 1941 reported from his position in the UK

Special Operations Executive that that organization had not yet sent any agents into the USSR or even begun training them, foreign intelligence headquarters in Moscow ("the Center") was disbelieving. Stalin himself became suspicious in 1942–44 when Philby repeatedly reported that there were *no* British spies in the USSR.[6] By October 1943 some analysts in the Center concluded that all of the "Cambridge Five"—who sent an enormous flow of valuable validated information—must have been double agents from the outset. Stalin eventually accepted the validity of the positive contributions of the Five while refusing to accept their reports that there were no British spies in the Soviet Union.[7]

The Center often dared not pass to Soviet leaders intelligence it feared would be unacceptable to them.[8] It withheld from Stalin and others an unknown portion of the materials submitted by the Cambridge Five and the "Red Orchestra" (the 1941–42 Soviet military intelligence network in Germany and Western Europe). Stalin harbored suspicions about his own intelligence officers abroad as well as about their agents, and he purged a number of those who, during the war, had served in the West.

Through an agent in the US Office of Strategic Services (OSS), the Soviets in 1943 obtained information purportedly on US contingency planning for possible military intervention into the territory of the Soviet Union in case of an impending or actual Soviet defeat, in order to counter the German army. A Soviet intelligence officer involved at the time has reported there were serious suspicions in Moscow that this plan, despite its hypothetical basis, represented an American design for possible intervention in the USSR under other circumstances.[9]

Toward the end of the war and immediately afterward, Soviet intelligence also obtained highly sensitive secret US and UK assessments of possible military measures to meet a potential Soviet threat, including contingency war plans involving employment of atomic weapons. Among the most important were British studies in 1944 by the secret Post-Hostilities Planning Committee, which envisaged the USSR as the main postwar adversary of the United Kingdom and explored opposing the Soviets militarily and using German forces. In the same category was a secret plan (Operation Unthinkable) for a worst-case contingency of war with the USSR in 1945 drawn up at Churchill's behest in May 1945 that envisaged use of a hundred thousand German troops.[10] Soviet military intelligence also obtained a copy of instructions from Churchill to Field Marshal Bernard Montgomery to collect and store German weapons for possible rearming of Germans to fight the Russians and learned that a skeleton staff and cadre for four divisions under a German general and officers (with British officers attached) had been established in the UK occupation zone. The United Kingdom also planned for a possible British airborne operation into Berlin if Germany surrendered to the West before Soviet troops arrived in Berlin. Additional British documents from 1945 through 1950 dealing with British and joint British-American assessments and contingency planning for possible hostilities with the Soviet Union were obtained by the Cambridge Five (mainly Guy Burgess) and were interpreted by Soviet intelligence analysts as threatening a possible Western attack.[11]

An official history of Russian foreign intelligence cites a September 1945 study by the US Joint Chiefs of Staff (JCS) as the first US document disclosing "plans for nuclear war" against the Soviet Union, "in which the USSR was already seen not as an ally but as enemy number one, against which war should be conducted with the employment of atomic weapons."[12] Soviet sources also contain varying accounts claiming knowledge of some or all of other US military contingency plans, but with a few exceptions these claims have not been confirmed. It is not known, for example, what the Soviets learned about a series of US contingency war plans prepared by the JCS from 1945 through 1950 that culminated in a plan called Dropshot (which envisaged a possible war in 1957 involving use of three hundred atomic weapons against two hundred Soviet cities and employment of 160 US and allied divisions against the USSR and its satellites in Eastern Europe).[13] Soviet intelligence was still trying unsuccessfully to obtain Dropshot in 1955–60.[14] When these plans were declassified and released by the US government in the 1970s (along with NSC-68), they became the subject of many commentaries by Soviet military and intelligence analysts alleging American responsibility for a militarized Cold War and Soviet effectiveness at frustrating such plans by enhancing Soviet military strength.[15]

Col. Aleksandr Feklisov, an intelligence officer who for many years served in both Washington and London (and headed the American desk in the Center in 1956–60), has said that when he was serving in London in 1949, the Soviet intelligence residency (*rezidentura*; station) there received top-secret plans of a US-UK joint staff group that concluded that the optimum time for an attack on the USSR would be 1952–53. Feklisov also (in 1994) cited a partial list of the then-declassified JCS contingency war plans from the late 1940s, but he did not claim that they had been obtained at the time. If they were in Soviet hands, they would have fed worst-case suspicions among Soviet leaders that American objectives included eradication of communism, dismemberment of the Soviet Union, and creation of successor states favorable to the United States.[16] Feklisov repeated the standard misconstrued portrayal of American references to 1952 (or 1952–53) as an "optimum" time of danger of outbreak of war, assuming and stating that this represented a predicted optimum time for a *US* attack on the USSR, whereas in fact it denoted a predicted US net assessment of the optimum time for a *Soviet* attack based on estimated Soviet attack capabilities.

Former KGB lieutenant general Pavel Sudoplatov, who was responsible in 1945–46 for intelligence on atomic weaponry and may have known that the US stockpile of atomic weapons in the late 1940s was small, has made a claim—which may be valid but has not been confirmed—that Stalin in 1947–48 knew the United States would not have a large enough atomic stockpile to destroy the Soviet Union before 1955.[17] Whether this was true or not—and surely Stalin assumed the United States would make contingency plans to use its atomic weapons—Stalin believed America was unlikely to launch a war against the Soviet Union in the near future unless provoked, and he maneuvered to maximize Soviet gains using measures well short of those that could lead to drastic American reactions.

Soviet intelligence reported to Stalin regularly on US and British intelligence and subversion activities directed against the USSR. Both intelligence officers and Stalin exaggerated such activities, which began as early as 1945 and greatly increased in 1949–54. There was plenty of information on real actions, including incursions into Soviet airspace, attempts to insert or recruit railway watchers, émigré-supported armed resistance in the western Ukraine, and a bogus communist-controlled underground resistance movement in Poland. A network of British-run agents clandestinely introduced into the Baltic states was taken over and used by Soviet counterintelligence, and fruitless US and British efforts to mount an insurgency in Albania were fully known to Soviet intelligence in advance (owing in part to Philby). The greatest impact of these largely ineffective Western efforts was to cement in Stalin's mind that the United States and the United Kingdom were indeed the USSR's main adversaries.[18]

As East-West tensions rose, Stalin observed the new American president, Harry Truman, whom he met at Potsdam in 1945, take a more assertive role, and he noted the American foreign policy establishment's interpretation of his February 1946 election speech to the Soviet people as a tocsin for a possible future military showdown between East and West.[19] By late 1946—even before the British handover of responsibility for Greece and Turkey to the United States in early 1947, precipitating the proclamation of the Truman Doctrine—Soviet intelligence assessments had reassigned the chief Western role in the Middle East to the United States.[20] *Pravda* interpreted Churchill's March 1946 "Iron Curtain" speech as a virtual ultimatum to accept Western domination or face war, and Stalin regarded it as significant that the speech was delivered in the United States with President Truman in attendance.[21] At about the same time, the American chargé d'affaires in Moscow, George Kennan, submitted in his famous February 1946 "Long Telegram" an analysis arguing that Soviet ideological conceptions postulating conflict precluded lasting compromises.[22] This had a powerful effect on policymaking in Washington.

Less well known, and less consequential, is a parallel analysis prepared in September 1946 by the Soviet ambassador to the United States, Nikolai Novikov. Novikov's analysis, requested by Foreign Minister Molotov and delivered on September 27, 1946, was a briefing on "US Foreign Policy in the Postwar Period" given to the Soviet delegation to the Foreign Ministers' Peace Conference meeting in Paris. When declassified and released in 1990, it was described as "in a way parallel to Kennan's famous cable," and in a way it was.[23] Novikov's opening sentence provided his key conclusion and reflected a Soviet leadership presumption: "The foreign policy of the United States, which reflects the imperialist tendencies of American monopolistic capital, is characterized in the postwar period by a striving for *world supremacy.*"[24] He argued that the United States had counted on sitting out the war while other powers would be destroyed or at least greatly weakened. He contended that greatly increased US military expenditures (exaggerating the point by comparing postwar US arms spending to 1938 levels) and far-flung bases around the globe "show clearly that a decisive role in the realization of plans for world dominance by the United States is played by its armed forces" and also "*the offensive nature of strategic concepts.*" He concluded by arguing that "*talk about a 'third [world] war'*, meaning a war against the Soviet Union, and even a direct call for this war—with the threat of using the atomic bomb" is an "attempt *to create an atmosphere of war psychosis* among the masses" and "*to prepare the conditions for winning world supremacy* in a new war, the date for which, to be sure, cannot be determined now by anyone, but which is contemplated by the most bellicose circles of American imperialism."[25] Although it did not play a role in setting Soviet policy, Novikov's briefing was an indication of thinking among Soviet leaders and an example of how Soviet diplomats and intelligence officers shaped their analyses to fit what those leaders (in this case Molotov) wanted to hear.

In September 1946 Secretary of State James Byrnes made clear in a speech that American troops would remain in Germany as long as the forces of the other countries remained there, confirming that President Roosevelt's statement to Stalin at Yalta that American troops would remain in Europe no more than two years after the end of the war no longer represented American policy (if it ever had). The United States also at that time confirmed a ban on releasing any economic reparations from the US occupation zone in Germany to the Soviet Union.

The last straw ending Stalin's hopes of collaborating with the West on his terms was the Marshall Plan. This was an instance where intelligence did influence Stalin. Materials from Soviet archives have shown that Stalin was initially hopeful that the US proposal could be made acceptable to Moscow if the United States were prepared to provide aid or loans without strings reinforcing future economic relations. As the meeting on the plan opened in June 1947, however, the Soviets learned from sources in London (principally Donald Maclean) that the United States and Britain had just agreed on using the Marshall Plan as a means to strengthen Western Europe against a perceived Soviet political threat and that American leaders envisaged long-term reciprocal commitments aimed at building up a European economic order with a strong US role.[26] Stalin changed course and suddenly attacked the proposal, insisting that interested Eastern European countries also not participate. The USSR's rejection of the plan and denial of participation by its disappointed dependencies further contributed to the division of Europe and ended Soviet hopes for collaboration with the Western powers.

By the fall of 1947, the Soviet evaluation of the main adversary had hardened to a point at which even Novikov's analysis was regarded as too soft. In a bold move probably inspired by Stalin himself, Counselor Tarasenko of the Soviet embassy in Washington on October 6, 1947, sent a message to Moscow attacking his ambassador's analysis for displaying superficial judgment and failing to assess accurately the motives behind American policy. This attack distorted Novikov's analysis, making it appear he had claimed that US policy was aimed only at intimidation, whereas he should have asserted that its goal was direct preparation for war against the USSR. Novikov was recalled from Washington and forced out of government service. Although the critique was unfair to Novikov, it accurately reflected the new, harder Soviet policy.[27]

Subsequent Soviet diplomatic and other analyses consistently stressed that America was preparing for a military confrontation and thus provided the rationale for Moscow's harsh diplomatic stance and increased military preparedness. This rationale, indeed, was no doubt the main purpose of the new hardened line. Stalin did not believe that a sudden American attack in the near future was likely, but intensified confrontation was looming, and he considered it necessary to generate support for countermeasures by picturing an easily understood threat.

In a September 1947 speech marking the founding of the Cominform (an association of leading European communist parties), Andrei Zhdanov reaffirmed the Soviet view of world politics as comprising two counterposed "camps," with the capitalist/imperialist camp headed by the United States. The key events affecting Soviet-American relations during the next three years—the Soviet blockade of West Berlin, the creation of the Federal Republic of Germany, the establishment of the North Atlantic Treaty Organization (NATO), the first Soviet atomic bomb test, the communist victory in China, and the outbreak of the Korean War—made Zhdanov's (and Stalin's) image a reality and militarized the confrontation between the two main adversaries.

A second wave of attempts to seize power by local communists on the periphery came in 1948. It was successful in Czechoslovakia but failed in Finland and in Greece (where it ended a civil war waged ever since December 1944 but now abandoned by Stalin).

The most serious attempt to unilaterally change the postwar formation of Eastern and Western blocs was the Soviet attempt to disrupt the integration of western Germany into the Western camp in an ill-starred land blockade of West Berlin in 1948–49—which failed owing to a successful Allied airlift and sanctions on trade with the USSR. Stalin finally abandoned the blockade and the attempt to remove western Berlin from the West and to prevent the emergence of the Federal Republic of Germany.

Neither the general hardening of Soviet policy nor Stalin's misjudgments in trying to blockade West Berlin in 1948 and unleashing the North Korean attack on South Korea in June 1950 rested on professional intelligence assessments. Their foundation instead was a set of distorted assumptions resulting from Stalin's application of an ideological lens in interpreting Western thinking and policy. This fault was not unique to Soviet intelligence and policymaking, but the extent of distortion was exceptional under Stalin's personal dictatorship.

Soviet intelligence, rather than moderating or correcting Stalin's misunderstanding of the West, reinforced it.[28] Lt. Gen. Vadim Kirpichenko, a former deputy chief of foreign intelligence in the KGB who served as deputy editor of an official six-volume study *Essays on the History of Russian Foreign Intelligence* published in the 1990s, notes with particular reference to Stalin's rejection of numerous intelligence reports warning of the impending Nazi attack in 1941 that "the leaders of the country had not required analytical information from the NKVD. They required, so to speak, 'fresh facts,' without any working over or context. What we received from sources of information we reported without any commentary or analysis." He further notes that at that time there was not any "informational or analytical service" in the main Soviet foreign intelligence organization, a condition that undercut the value of its intelligence reporting to Stalin and Molotov. He dryly states that, "in general, on the eve of the war the Soviet leaders did not accord our Service high State significance."[29] Indeed, the principal Soviet intelligence analyst was Stalin, who in the 1930s reportedly had said, "Don't tell me what you think. Give me the facts and the source!"[30] Despite Stalin's bias, steps were taken after the war to build a still constrained but at least professional analytical capability in processing foreign intelligence, including in the departments of the Central Committee of the Communist Party concerned with foreign affairs as well as in the intelligence services.[31]

Kennan commented in his Long Telegram in 1946 on "the unsolved mystery as to who, if anyone, in the Soviet Union actually receives accurate and unbiased information about the outside world. . . . I for one am reluctant to believe that Stalin himself receives anything like an objective picture of the outside world." In another message, Kennan noted that Stalin was subject to constant "misinformation and misinterpretations about us and our policies" from his advisers.[32] Stalin, of course, was responsible for this situation and indeed enforced it. Below the top political level, there were biases in collecting, selecting, and transmitting information to Stalin and his top advisers, as well as competition among the several intelligence services and important elements of the government and Communist Party.

The Soviet leadership undertook steps to improve intelligence assessments just as the Cold War got fully under way, and the United States was firmly established in 1946 as the USSR's main adversary. In May 1947, on Foreign Minister Molotov's recommendation, the several foreign intelligence services—the foreign intelligence arm (*Pervoe glavnoe upravlenyie*, or PGU) of the Ministry of State Security (MGB), the Main Intelligence Directorate (GRU) of the General Staff in the Ministry of Defense, and the International Information Department (OMI) of the Central Committee—were combined into a single Committee on Information (KI) headed by Molotov. The arrangement did not sit well with either the state security or military elements or the organizations from which they had been detached, and the military component was returned to the General Staff in January 1949. In February the KI itself was resubordinated from the Council of Ministers to the Foreign Ministry. Molotov turned over his responsibility to senior deputy minister Andrei Vyshinsky (who in turn shunned the responsibility, delegating it to another deputy minister, Yakov Malik, and later Valerian Zorin). In the field, KI residencies were subordinated to Soviet ambassadors, and in some cases the ambassador himself (including, notably, Ambassador Aleksandr S. Panyushkin in Washington) assumed also the position of chief of the KI residency.[33]

In November 1951 the KI was disbanded and foreign intelligence, the PGU, was reestablished in the MGB (after 1954, the KGB). A "Small KI," an autonomous organization with overall analytical responsibilities, remained affiliated with the Foreign Ministry until 1958 and vied with the reestablished state security and military intelligence services to get its information to the leadership first. In 1958 it was transferred to become the Information Service of the Central Committee.

The KI and Small KI experiment included the creation of a combined, if short-lived, analytical service that brought in a number of young new intelligence analysts with a less parochial bent than most of those from state security and the military, although initially with little knowledge of the West. A number of them later became influential diplomats, including Georgy Kornienko, the long-serving senior deputy to Andrei Gromyko, and such international relations experts as Valentin Falin, Viktor Karpov, and Lev Mendelyevich, all of whom became senior advisers and ambassadors. These men all later played a part in developing a more nuanced Soviet understanding of Western adversaries.

The archives of the Small KI make clear that the KI integrated and analyzed intelligence information and sometimes provided useful reports to the political leadership, albeit always tailored to be politically and ideologically correct, especially if they related to the main adversary. The leadership was free to accept or ignore them, and the latter attitude was all too frequently the case. For example, the KI correctly understood the situation in Iran in 1952 and knew of the US and British plotting to replace Prime Minister Mohammed Mossadeq, but Stalin and Molotov regarded Mossadeq as an

American collaborator and dismissed reports of American plotting against him, believing that the United States was playing a game to replace British influence and advance American oil monopolies *through* Mossadeq.[34]

From the early years of the Cold War, Soviet intelligence collection activities were targeted principally on the policies and plans of the Western powers, above all on the United States. Recruitments of Westerners declined sharply with the end of World War II, and wartime assets disappeared or lost their access to valuable information.[35] Nonetheless, after 1948 Soviet intelligence built extensive new espionage networks, not only in the United Kingdom and the United States but also in Japan, France, West Germany, and elsewhere in Europe (after 1949 particularly in member countries of NATO).[36] In Moscow, after the defection of several key agents, a special Politburo commission headed by Georgy Malenkov and including Lavrenty Beria of the NKVD and GRU chief Fyodor Kuznetsov reviewed the competence of the intelligence services, each of which sought to find fault with its rivals.[37] These efforts notwithstanding, it is difficult to find evidence of any significant contribution Soviet intelligence made to the basic understanding of the United States and its major allies held by Stalin and other Soviet leaders.

In March 1951 the KI formally confirmed the United States as its main adversary, emphasizing that intelligence on US capabilities, intentions, and actions would be the fundamental task of foreign intelligence work over a long period of time (the designation indeed remained in place until 1990).[38]

In November–December 1952 Stalin made preparations to consolidate further the intelligence and counterintelligence organizations, and although the reorganization was approved by the Politburo (then termed the Presidium) at the end of December, implementation was abandoned after Stalin's death in early March 1953. During the deliberations on the planned reorganization, Stalin referred to the United States as "our main enemy" (*glavnyi nash vrag*), an even stronger variant on the intelligence service's designation of the United States as "the main adversary"—a term, incidentally, never known to have been used by any Soviet political leader.[39]

Andrei Gromyko, who was in charge of the Small KI in the mid-1950s, saw to it that the Foreign Ministry played a major role in intelligence assessment (Molotov had done this as well). In a passage added to an edition of the official *History of Diplomacy* revised under his leadership, he noted that governments now have "numerous channels and means of acquiring information" but asserted that "the most authoritative source of information for every government are the materials of the diplomatic establishment, its proposals and recommendations." An important function of embassies, he stated, was to "accumulate information on the situation in the world, in particular countries and regions" and "show the objective causes of developing processes, to have perspectives and thus act on finding ways and opportunities to affect the regulation of budding conflictual situations and also the stimulation of the development of positive tendencies." He also called for "objectivity of analysis" on all developments around the world.[40]

None of the improvements in intelligence analysis, or in espionage or other intelligence collection, had discernible impact on Stalin's headstrong personal role in interpreting events and deciding policies. At the end Stalin turned inward, connecting paranoid fears of plots by external adversaries with dark concerns about his colleagues. He became suspicious that the ever-loyal Molotov was in league with the Central Intelligence Agency (CIA), that crony Marshal Kliment Voroshilov had for years been a British agent, and that longtime colleagues Malenkov, Beria, and Anastas Mikoyan also merited close watching. A prospective purge of many of his closest colleagues was stillborn when he died on March 5, 1953.[41]

CHAPTER TWO

Khrushchev

Thaw and Crisis, 1954–64

Nikita Khrushchev gradually moved into a leading position in the collective leadership that took power following Stalin's death and became fully dominant by 1957, when he managed to oust a majority of Politburo members he labeled the "Anti-Party Group." The new leaders shared Stalin's Marxist-Leninist worldview but showed sharply varying readiness to consider departures in some areas of policy. Georgy Malenkov moved early to advocate mutual deterrence and peaceful coexistence, only to have Khrushchev ally himself with Vyacheslav Molotov and other conservatives to attack his initiatives and overwhelm him politically—albeit later to adopt those views as his own and the Communist Party line. Meanwhile, the American adversary cautiously sought to sound out the new Soviet leadership.

President Dwight Eisenhower, who had assumed office only six weeks before Stalin's death, was disinclined to take any initiative toward the Soviet Union. British prime minister Winston Churchill (again in that office), however, took the initiative by proposing publicly on May 11 that the Western leaders meet with the Soviet leaders at "the summit" (coining the term that would be used for decades thereafter). The Soviet leaders had an equivocal reaction.[1] Eisenhower himself was wary of such a meeting before the views of the new leaders in Moscow were clarified, believing public opinion could have excessive optimistic expectations. Eisenhower was, however, more ready than Secretary of State John Foster Dulles to test the Soviet position, and on April 16, 1954, in a speech called "The Chance for Peace," he set out four preliminary conditions that the Soviet leaders could meet to demonstrate their readiness to "strengthen world trust."[2] The four were signature of an Austrian peace treaty, release of World War II prisoners of war still held, an armistice in Korea, and steps to curb the arms race. Within two years, the first three of these were fully met, and the Soviet leaders had shown readiness to reach agreements in the fourth area by agreeing (in May 1955) in principle to reduce arms and accept inspection in Europe.

One of the new Soviet leaders took an initiative to recognize new imperatives of the nuclear age. On August 8, 1953, Georgy Malenkov, now the chairman of the Council of Ministers (prime minister), announced that the United States no longer had a monopoly on the hydrogen bomb, the Soviet Union having just held its first test of a partial thermonuclear bomb. But in seeking to present a step toward military equality with the United States, Malenkov again called for the peaceful resolution of any contested issues, stating that "we consider that there are no objective grounds for a clash between the United States and the USSR." Although not a departure from previous Soviet positions, it reemphasized the importance of peaceful resolution of differences with the main adversary.[3]

Then, in a significant departure from the previous Soviet position, a year after Stalin's death—on March 12, 1954—Malenkov declared that a world war in the nuclear age "would mean the end of world civilization," a statement echoing what President Eisenhower had stated on December 8, 1953. On the same day, his Politburo colleague Anastas Mikoyan added that nuclear weapons in Soviet hands served "as a means for deterring aggressors and for waging peace," for the first time explicitly ascribing a deterrent role for Soviet nuclear weapons. Malenkov's statement directly, and Mikoyan's indirectly, not only contradicted the logic of the Stalinist doctrine on inevitability of war but also were arguably not consistent with predictions of ultimate victory for socialism in the world.[4] These statements even raised the intriguing possibility that those issues had arisen while Stalin was still in power. Stalin, in his last theoretical pronouncement some six months before his death, had written that "some comrades," not identified, believed that "wars between capitalist countries have ceased to be inevitable. . . . These comrades are mistaken. . . . They say that the theories of Lenin that imperialism inevitably gives rise to war must be considered obsolete. . . . That is incorrect." Stalin also had continued to publicly display optimism as to the outcome of a nuclear world war, should one occur: "War with the USSR would certainly pose the question of the continued existence of capitalism itself"—but not, apparently, the existence of the Soviet Union.[5]

Malenkov's bold revisionism put him in a politically vulnerable position, and his opponents forced him a year later to retract his statement and used the issue to remove him from the post of chairman of the Council of Ministers in February 1955, although he (like Molotov) remained on the Politburo (Presidium). But the Twentieth Communist Party Congress in February 1956, most famously remembered for Khrushchev's denunciation of Stalin's crimes, revised Stalinist doctrine to conclude that "there is no fatal inevitability of war." And the Twenty-Second Communist Party Congress in 1961 fully embraced the Malenkov heresy: A nuclear war "would cause the complete destruction of the main centers of civilization and the annihilation of entire peoples. . . . A contemporary nuclear war, however one looks at it, can in no way be a factor that would accelerate the revolution and bring nearer the victory of socialism"; "only madmen could want such a catastrophe to happen."[6]

Recognition of the implications of a dawning nuclear age did not change the belief in Moscow (or Washington) of a continuing contest between the two main adversaries. But it did call for consideration of possible means of reducing tensions and the possibility of war, while continuing to prevent the adversary from threatening one's own security and to seek ways of achieving one's own objectives. As Khrushchev consolidated his authority within the leadership, not only was the inevitability of war in the nuclear age abandoned, but also at the same time (at the Twentieth Communist Party Congress) a significant new formulation to describe a possible, and desirable, relationship between the capitalist and socialist camps was unveiled: "peaceful coexistence." Peaceful coexistence did not mean an end to the Cold War, but it envisaged that the conflict between the two sides—a conflict the Soviet leaders still believed would eventually be won by socialism triumphant in the entire world—would be won by the ineluctable victory of "the working class" (which had power in the Soviet Union) over the capitalist rulers of the imperialist states. This victory would, however, as originally projected by Karl Marx, be historically destined rather than the result of war. Many in the West considered peaceful coexistence to be a propaganda slogan designed to mask continuing Soviet pursuit of world domination, but it was not. To be sure, it was used in propaganda, but its real significance was an ideologically sanctioned recognition of realism in the nuclear age.[7]

Khrushchev and other Soviet leaders continued to believe that Western leaders were hostile to the USSR and endorsed as a corollary of peaceful coexistence the maintenance of a strong Soviet nuclear and overall military deterrent in order to prevent Western resort to force. Although Soviet leaders embraced the idea that war was not inevitable and that military conflict with America should if possible be averted, war remained a deadly possibility if not prevented by diplomacy and military strength.

In response to interest on both sides in reducing tensions, the first East-West summit meeting since the Potsdam summit in July 1945 convened in Geneva in July 1955. Western leaders quickly saw that Khrushchev was the most important of the several Soviet leaders who attended, including the colorless Nikolai Bulganin, who had succeeded Malenkov as chairman of the Council of Ministers and was the nominal head of the Soviet delegation. Marshal Georgy Zhukov, minister of defense, who had recently been added to the party Presidium (as the Politburo was then called), was also included for the first time that a military member of the leadership played a political or diplomatic role. He had in 1946 visited the United States for a World War II victory celebration and been escorted by Gen. Dwight Eisenhower. So they met again.

Although no concrete agreements were reached, the Soviet leaders gained confidence, with Khrushchev in particular bolstered by a belief he had taken the measure of his foreign adversaries. He later stated that the meeting had convinced him and his colleagues that "our enemies probably feared us as much as we feared them" and that it was "an important breakthrough for us on the diplomatic front. We had established ourselves as able to hold our own in the international arena."[8] Ambassador Charles Bohlen believed that the Geneva summit led Khrushchev to conclude the West was not planning to attack the Soviet Union.[9] The now-declassified briefing papers prepared before the meeting by Foreign Ministry / KI analysts were professionally done (although they did not know about President Eisenhower's "Open Skies" proposal). The KI also had analysts on hand who worked with intelligence officers supplying intercepted communications during the conference.[10]

The Soviet leaders were always suspicious of American instigation of subversion in Eastern Europe, but they recognized that the internal crises in East Germany in 1953 and in Poland and Hungary in 1956 arose from domestic problems and did not fear direct Western intervention.

Khrushchev's aggressive diplomatic ventures owed nothing to intelligence; they resulted from his impetuous nature, faith in the political power of nuclear weapons, ideological view of world politics, and lack of understanding of the West. He gambled with nuclear brinkmanship in the Suez Crisis of 1956. Lacking appropriate means to aid Egypt, which had been led to expect Soviet support, Khrushchev publicized a Soviet message to the British and French governments warning that if they did not cease their intervention, nuclear missiles could strike their countries. The Soviets had no missiles deployed capable of such a strike, and Britain and France called off their intervention because of American insistence (and an acute financial crisis caused by absence of American support), not owing to Khrushchev's threat.[11] But judging from indications in internal Soviet discussions and the testimony of his son Sergei, Khrushchev believed that his threat had led to the Anglo-French withdrawal.[12]

In June 1957 Khrushchev definitively defeated his erstwhile colleagues in the post-Stalin collective leadership, who were subsequently branded "the anti-party group." Marshal Zhukov, whose support to Khrushchev had been important in defeating Malenkov, Molotov, and the other political rivals, publicly pledged support to the new Khrushchev party leadership "on behalf of the armed forces." But if Zhukov could pledge the support of the armed forces for one political leader, he might do so for another. In October, while Zhukov was on an official visit abroad, he was suddenly relieved of all his military and political posts, sharply criticized, and retired permanently from political life.[13]

At about the same time, Khrushchev's attraction to the use of nuclear bluff and blackmail was boosted by the USSR's first successful test of an intercontinental ballistic missile and orbiting of *Sputnik*, the first artificial satellite of Earth. The alarmed Western reaction to those developments magnified the strategic significance of Soviet entry into the missile age and encouraged Khrushchev to seek political advantages from the promise of strength even long before significant military capabilities were achieved. At one point, he talked about Soviet missiles being "turned out like sausages," with seeming disregard for the possibility that such threats might lead the other side to respond in kind.

In October 1957 Khrushchev spun a tale of a Turkish and NATO threat to intervene in Syria and announced military maneuvers, then claimed credit for forestalling a NATO attack on Syria that was never contemplated. In July 1958 the pro-Western king and prime minister of Iraq were killed and succeeded by a military dictator who was considered a threat by its neighbors. In response to their appeals for assistance, the United States landed troops in Lebanon and the United Kingdom in Jordan. The Soviet Union with fanfare announced military maneuvers in the Transcaucasus and Bulgaria and issued vague warnings against a Western intervention in Iraq that was never contemplated. Soon thereafter, in September 1958, Khrushchev again issued verbal threats as a supportive gesture to the Chinese communists, who were bombarding the Nationalist-held island of Quemoy, and claimed to have prevented an American intervention. In fact, the United States never contemplated such an intervention (nor did the Chinese leaders welcome this unsought "support"). But then his run of successful bluffs ran out.

Khrushchev's confidence became his nemesis in a crisis that he initiated in November 1958 when he called for the Western powers to withdraw their military and political presence from West Berlin, to convert it into a "free city," and to recognize the German Democratic Republic (East Germany). In messages to the Western powers soon after, the initiative was broadened to include a six-month deadline for signing a German peace treaty with both German states (constituting Western diplomatic recognition of East Germany, which the Western powers were not prepared to do). Khrushchev had important defensive objectives: to force Western recognition of East Germany, to stop the massive exodus of East Germans through West Berlin, and to curtail extensive Western intelligence operations mounted through Berlin. As he later put it, Berlin was "a bone in my throat," and he sought to remove it. He also had important offensive goals: to end a Western presence deep in Eastern Europe and to do so by coercive diplomacy in order to emphasize Soviet politico-military strength and weaken the political stature of the United States, West Germany, and NATO. He sought to shift the "correlation of forces" in the USSR's favor and saw West Berlin as a vulnerable Western pressure point.

The ensuing Berlin Crisis lasted four years, finally ending with no change in the city's status. Inept and damaging, Khrushchev's failed initiative stemmed entirely from his overconfidence in judging that the main adversary and its allies would acquiesce in such a political defeat. In launching the venture, Khrushchev had obtained the consent of his compliant colleagues without seeking any intelligence advice on possible Western reactions.[14] He was aware of budding American concern as to a possible "missile gap" favoring the USSR, and he may have thought he could play that US perception to his advantage. If so, the calculation failed. Although US concern about Soviet missile strength did grow during 1959–60 when Berlin was a focal point of US-Soviet confrontation and contributed to a sense of crisis, during 1961 it became clear to all that America actually had the lead in strategic missiles. By then Khrushchev realized that his Berlin ploy had become a liability rather than a lever and settled in August 1961 for cutting off westward emigration of East Germans (and sharply curtailing Western intelligence operations) by unilaterally building the infamous Berlin Wall.

What altered Khrushchev's view of America during the crisis was the firmness of the US and NATO stand, which was reported by Soviet intelligence, but also by a change in his own impressions of the United States and its leaders. His twenty-day visit to the United States in September 1959—the first ever by a Soviet leader—provided him with a partial corrective and broadening of his understanding of the United States. Upon his return to the Soviet Union, he publicly stated his belief that President Eisenhower "sincerely wishes to see the end of the Cold War." Khrushchev saw his reception in America (he received full honors as head of state although he did not hold that title) as according himself personally, and by extension the USSR, equality with President Eisenhower and the United States, in his eyes reflecting a major advance.

There had been unprecedented high-level visits on both sides in 1959 leading up to Khrushchev's visit and a planned return visit by President Eisenhower to the USSR. The two first deputy premiers of the USSR, Anastas Mikoyan and Frol Kozlov, came to the United States in January and July, and Vice President Richard Nixon visited Moscow in July and August. These were useful familiarization visits rather than vehicles for diplomatic negotiations, although Mikoyan did recommend to Eisenhower that the two sides work to "end the cold war."[15]

Intelligence had little influence on Khrushchev's basic views toward the United States. His political power allowed him to disregard intelligence he received or even not to consult his intelligence services, and he relied instead on his own limited direct observations and personal judgments. The KGB lacked high-grade sources of political intelligence on the main adversary that could correct Khrushchev's misperceptions. For example, KGB foreign intelligence reported extensively on events in 1960, but apart from such things as acquiring Western position papers prepared for the aborted May 1960 Paris summit, various Western diplomatic exchanges on Berlin and Germany, and a steady stream of documents and reports on NATO planning, there was nothing of note on high-level political decision making in Washington in the annual report covering 1960 sent to Khrushchev by the head of the KGB in early 1961.[16]

Khrushchev believed that CIA director Allen Dulles was responsible for sending the U-2 reconnaissance plane that was shot down after penetrating far into Soviet airspace on May 1, 1960. Thinking that President Eisenhower would not have authorized the flight, Khrushchev sought a propaganda dividend by suddenly producing the pilot, who had survived the event, and publicly suggesting that anti-Soviet American militarists and intelligence chiefs had been responsible for the flight. Rather than exonerating Eisenhower, however, the statement implied that the president did not control American government actions—a charge he could not let stand—and led him to assert publicly his own responsibility. When Eisenhower than refused to offer an apology that Khrushchev had demanded, Khrushchev canceled his participation in a planned Four Power summit already convening in Paris and called off the Eisenhower visit to the Soviet Union planned for June. This episode, marked by Soviet misperceptions and propaganda overreach, in effect suspended US-Soviet relations until the change of administration in Washington in January 1961.[17]

John F. Kennedy, Andrei Gromyko told Khrushchev, would be anti-Soviet like his father. KGB analysts on the other hand believed that he would try to moderate tensions. Both, however, thought that Kennedy believed in a missile gap in Soviet favor as he had highlighted in his election campaign and would therefore pursue a military buildup.[18] Khrushchev, eager to test the young new president's mettle over Berlin, sought an early meeting with him.

In a January 1961 speech before Kennedy's inauguration, Khrushchev made clear that war must be prevented, not only general nuclear war but also even local, limited, conventional wars involving the great powers. But he also seemed to promise stepped-up Soviet support for "wars of national liberation" in previously colonial territories such as South Vietnam, the Democratic Republic of the Congo, and Algeria, wars he depicted as just and inevitable, although not appropriate for direct great-power intervention. Kennedy and his advisers interpreted the speech as articulating a challenge the West had to meet. Khrushchev, who did not intend or see his remarks in that light, was (we now know) dismayed by the negative US reaction and felt personally rebuffed by Kennedy.[19]

The failed American landing of anti-Castro Cuban émigrés at the Bay of Pigs in April 1961 also affected Khrushchev's view of Kennedy. The Soviet leader believed that Kennedy had been inveigled into the venture by Allen Dulles and Secretary of the Treasury Douglas Dillon, holdover Republicans from the Eisenhower administration.[20] The move affected the very kind of newly liberated country Khrushchev had touted in his January speech. It also contributed to Khrushchev's perception of Kennedy as a young and inexperienced leader without a firm hand on foreign policy, a view not changed by their personal meeting in Vienna in June. On that occasion, Khrushchev tried to browbeat Kennedy, and the two leaders largely talked past one another in sterile debate fashion rather than resolving or clarifying their differences. Khrushchev's development of respect for Kennedy as an opponent would have to await subsequent events.

Khrushchev's and Kennedy's use of unofficial, off-the-record personal communication channels, which bypassed some bureaucratic filters and were unlikely to leak, bore mixed results in terms of building mutual understanding. Even before his inauguration, Kennedy had used a KGB officer posing as a Soviet newsman in Washington to pass a message that he would be firm but was willing to seek common ground on Berlin. In May he used a GRU officer ostensibly serving as an embassy press officer, Col. Georgy Bol'shakov, who became a conduit through White House press secretary Pierre Salinger and soon through the president's brother Robert. Although this channel was used to help defuse a crisis in Berlin later in 1961, Khrushchev abused it in 1962 to give Kennedy false assurances that the USSR would not send missiles to Cuba, thereby ending the arrangement. Kennedy nevertheless moved to establish another such channel in September 1963 through Col. Georgy Karpovich, a KGB officer, but it ended almost immediately with Kennedy's demise.[21]

Khrushchev sometimes benefited from concrete and verifiable intelligence information as he conducted his proactive, erratic diplomacy. Throughout the 1960s Soviet intelligence obtained good coverage of NATO planning, including policy discussions and concrete military plans for various contingencies concerning Berlin. For example, KGB chairman Aleksandr Shelepin was able in July 1961 to report to Khrushchev that NATO was preparing to deal with the Berlin Crisis as a military problem with serious contingency planning and also considering various possible sanctions against the USSR and East Germany. Stiff personal letters on US resolve sent by President Kennedy to the leaders of Britain, France, and West Germany as well as follow-up actions by Secretary of State Dean Rusk were all intercepted and rapidly reported to Moscow. Also, an American sergeant stationed at the Orly Armed Forces Crisis Center in Paris was handling, and copying for Moscow, all the NATO top-secret Live Oak military contingency planning documents for the Berlin Crisis, and there were multiple other penetrations of NATO.[22]

At the same time, Khrushchev was, according to his son, wary and dismissive of intelligence reports from vague, undisclosed sources and possible hostile misinformation, perhaps because he himself had authorized intelligence disinformation and deception measures.[23] In June 1960 the KGB had sent him a report that its chief in Washington had received information from "contact maintained with a [NATO] collaborator of the CIA" that "the Pentagon has prepared a plan for a preventive nuclear strike on the USSR while the USA has a preponderance of strategic arms." According to the cursory and ambiguous account we have on this report (the original document is not available), it would appear at most that allegedly someone was *proposing* consideration of a preventive strike while the United States had a clear strategic advantage, not that one was planned. There is no indication that this report received serious attention in Moscow.[24] In early 1962 a GRU report was said to describe a list of Soviet cities targeted by American missiles, ready for immediate launch if and when ordered.[25] Another GRU report in March 1962 stated that, "according to a source in the US national security bureaucracy," in June 1961 after the Vienna summit the Pentagon had given serious consideration to a nuclear strike on the USSR but had called it off after a Soviet nuclear weapons test in September showed that Soviet thermonuclear weapons were more advanced than Americans had previously believed.[26] Such alarmist reports may have sustained preexisting suspicions in the minds of Soviet leaders, but they did not lead to serious consideration that America was ruled by leaders bent on radical gambles.

Khrushchev had decided long before that American leaders, specifically including Eisenhower and John Foster Dulles, and then Kennedy, were rational and did not intend to start a war or launch a surprise nuclear attack on the Soviet Union. He had earlier believed Kennedy and NATO would back down over Berlin, but in October 1961 he abandoned the idea of signing a separate peace treaty with East Germany (and also suspended earlier plans to send substantial arms, including air-defense missiles, to Cuba).[27] At a meeting of the

Presidium (the renamed Politburo) on January 8, 1962, Khrushchev admitted to his colleagues that he had been wrong in believing that Kennedy would give in on Berlin, asserting that Kennedy was in a weaker position than he had thought and that leading capitalist circles were calling the tune on US policy. He also acknowledged that the Western Europeans had been more supportive of a strong Berlin stand than he had anticipated. In the future, he said, the USSR would still press on Berlin but without ultimatums.[28] Khrushchev's more sober views at the end of 1961 were probably also induced by an important October speech by Deputy Secretary of Defense Roswell Gilpatric asserting that the United States had such strategic superiority that it could respond to any Soviet attack with an even more powerful response than the initial Soviet attack (the USSR had only four intercontinental ballistic missile launchers operationally deployed at the time). Khrushchev made no riposte like his earlier bragging about Soviet missiles being "turned out like sausages," and indeed no Soviet challenge to Gilpatric's assertion was issued at all.

The earlier back-and-forth in the United States on missile gaps and the strategic balance had shown the importance of perceptions and the problematic nature of communicating information as to military capabilities and intentions. A potentially serious moment in October 1961 provides an example of how even tactical events can affect mutual understanding. Over the period October 22 to 28, a minicrisis arose over the issue of Western access to East Berlin. East German guards at a sector-crossing point called "Checkpoint Charlie" refused to allow the American civilian deputy commandant to enter East Berlin without showing identification documents. US authorities misperceived this action as an attempt by Moscow to squeeze the West into indirect recognition of East German sovereignty in East Berlin and thus as a threat to the American presence and authority in West Berlin and to reciprocal rights of access to all parts of the city. Fearing the consequences of backing down, the United States brought in American troops to escort the official into East Berlin, and the East German guards withdrew. Eventually the

Americans brought in tanks, including some with bulldozer attachments, to clear away obstacles that might be placed at the checkpoint, and the Soviets met this step by bringing in their own tanks. A stalemate with ten uncovered tank guns on each side pointing at the other ended only when President Kennedy contacted Khrushchev through Colonel Bol'shakov and suggested that if the Soviets withdrew their tanks, the Americans would do the same. This happened, the East Germans abandoned their identification demand, and the status quo ante was restored.[29]

The difference in American and Soviet interpretations of what had occurred was stunning. The American side, including President Kennedy, was satisfied the outcome meant the Soviet leadership had understood American determination and backed down. The United States had stood fast and won. Khrushchev, for his part, believed *he* had won. Unlike the Americans, he knew he had not instigated the credentials demand (the East Germans had done it on their own), and when the Americans introduced tanks, he thought they were using a contrived issue to challenge the recently established Berlin Wall. To him, the Soviet response had successfully rebuffed a major American initiative to use military force to intervene in the Soviet sphere. In his taped memoir, he says the outcome was "a great victory for us": "The West had tested our nerve by prodding us with the barrels of their [tank] cannons and found us ready to accept their challenge. They learned that they couldn't frighten us."[30]

Specific and accurate intelligence on the Soviet side played an important part in leading Khrushchev to his conclusion about the outcome. Soviet military intelligence had observed and photographed tanks *equipped with bulldozer attachments* practicing techniques to break down part of a replica Berlin Wall in a secluded wooded area of West Berlin. Gen. Lucius Clay, a hero of the 1948 Berlin confrontation who had recently been returned to Berlin as a symbol of steadfastness, had undertaken the exercise. Although no one in Washington was even aware of Clay's action, Khrushchev and the other Soviet leaders, thanks to Soviet intelligence reporting, had been fully informed about it. Little wonder that Khrushchev connected the American tanks at the checkpoint with possible actions directed at the wall. The lesson for intelligence, and for recipient use of intelligence, was that accurate information, while in general a good thing, can be wrongly interpreted. In this instance, US practice for a military contingency was misconstrued in Moscow as preparation for a hostile initiative.[31]

As was often the case throughout the Cold War, intelligence in the Checkpoint Charlie case was not up to the task of clarifying the intentions of the other side. Neither side had political intelligence on the other sufficient to provide reliable understanding of the other's initiatives. The problem of accurately communicating intentions, and the related problems of unintended communication of intentions and of communication of apparent but not real intentions, are all difficult and made yet more so by inability to know whether one's real intentions have been understood by an adversary when the communication is intended or whether inaccurate understanding of one's intentions has inadvertently occurred. The situation becomes even more uncertain when secret intelligence conveys inaccurate information or when misinformation and deception are involved, and even accurate but partial intelligence can reinforce misperceptions or otherwise aggravate misunderstandings.

In some respects, Soviet intelligence can fairly be said to have played a positive role. Soviet and other Warsaw Pact espionage penetrations of NATO headquarters and NATO member countries were extensive during virtually all of the Cold War. Potentially most important for a war that fortunately never occurred, these disclosures of secret NATO political and military deliberations and decisions revealed thinking, plans, and decisions relating to a whole range of East-West relations. Although such information might on occasion be exploited for unilateral advantage, overall it conveyed in a way that open Western declarations could not the firmness of the Western position (in the case of Berlin, it contributed to the Soviet decision to drop ultimatums). It also provided evidence that NATO had no offensive plans for war against the Warsaw Pact—although Soviet intelligence remained suspicious that the United States had ultra-secret offensive war plans not shared with its NATO partners and thus not attainable by Soviet espionage against NATO and its member countries. On the whole, Warsaw Pact intelligence on NATO probably actually served basic Western interests.[32]

Regrettably, in some cases Soviet intelligence obtained information that was interpreted by intelligence analysts and military leaders as representing American and NATO offensive intentions. In the documentary intelligence provided to the West by Col. Oleg Penkovsky were assessments by Col. Gen. Semyon Ivanov, the chief of the Operations Directorate of the Soviet General Staff, of two major NATO field exercises held in 1959 and 1960. In both cases, although the exercises were announced to be for NATO defensive responses, the actual scenarios as reported to Moscow showed NATO forces launching nuclear strikes *before* the Warsaw Pact attack. Ivanov characterized the acknowledged defensive purposes as meant to mislead NATO publics and military officers and concluded that the exercises revealed intentions for NATO at some time to launch a surprise attack claiming it was a preemptive defensive response. Thus the Soviet military leadership was given top-secret intelligence analyses, buttressed with detailed facts, seeming to support US and NATO first-strike plans and intentions.[33]

Soviet intelligence reports often exaggerated the Western military threat through deductive reasoning based on assumptions of hostile intent rather than evidence. As we have noted, Soviet leaders often discounted such reports because they understood the bureaucratic impulses of those supplying them and had taken their own measure of Western leaders via direct contacts, an important positive factor that helped keep the Cold War cold.

As the Berlin Crisis wound down and the American edge in strategic military power grew, Soviet leaders became even more convinced that nuclear war had to be prevented. At the Twenty-Second Communist Party Congress in October 1961, the Communist Party of the Soviet Union (CPSU) replaced Lenin's party program of 1919 with a new one that confirmed the absolute need for peaceful coexistence in the nuclear age.[34]

This reaffirmation of a vitally important guideline did not, however, prevent Khrushchev from embarking on what would turn out to be his most dangerous foreign policy initiative, secretly deploying in Cuba nuclear-armed missiles that could at least temporarily shore up the weak Soviet strategic missile force in the strategic balance with the United States. The origin of this initiative was Khrushchev's misunderstanding of a remark made to his son-in-law and informal foreign affairs adviser, Aleksei Adzhubei, by President Kennedy. Meeting Adzhubei on November 25, Kennedy said that American concern over Castro's Cuba could be compared with Soviet concern over developments in Hungary in 1956 that had been settled in three days. Presumably he was trying to say that the United States wanted to handle Cuba less drastically than the USSR had dealt with the uprising in Hungary. Unfortunately, Khrushchev interpreted the comment as indicating that Kennedy thought he had a right to deal with Cuba quickly and forcefully (as indeed he had unsuccessfully tried to do earlier in the year). The Soviet leaders were well aware of the American program of subversion and sabotage in Cuba mounted after the Bay of Pigs fiasco, and they interpreted Kennedy's remark as warning them that he intended to act again to remove Castro and that they should not stand in the way.[35]

Khrushchev consequently revived a plan to provide arms to Cuba that he had suspended the previous fall, and in the spring of 1962 the Presidium first decided to send weapons to the Cuban armed forces and later decided also to include, under Soviet control and with Soviet protective forces, tactical nuclear weapons for defense of Cuba and strategic missiles with nuclear warheads capable of striking deep into the United States.[36] Khrushchev pushed through this reckless move with the support of the military establishment, believing that the deployment could be made secretly so he could present the United States and the world with a fait accompli in November

1962 after the US elections. He believed that Kennedy, however un-happily and reluctantly, would acquiesce in the deployment. Once again he miscalculated, overestimating (with no professional assessment) that US intelligence would not learn of the action until after the US election in November and underestimating his adversary's mettle. Once again he was compelled to retreat.[37] The only gains he achieved were a conditional American promise not to invade Cuba and an American statement (not made public) reaffirming its intention to remove its missiles from Turkey.

Khrushchev embarked on this gambit, as he had with Berlin, without seeking any intelligence assessment as to likely or possible American responses or other potential international developments, or as to whether the deployments could be successfully concealed. (Gromyko tried to raise questions about possible American reactions but fell silent when it became clear that Khrushchev did not want to hear them.) As for Soviet intelligence, it did not discover that the United States had known of the missile deployment for an entire week, during which time American leaders considered, decided upon, and prepared for a course of action. During the crisis, Soviet military intelligence did provide detailed data on the US military buildup and readiness for possible action, confirming American resolve. As for high policy, there was no intelligence information on either side from espionage or other means concerning the deliberations, decisions, and intentions of the leaders prior to or during the crisis. Thus, on crucial questions of perceptions and willpower, the leaders of the two adversaries had to consider and select their successive actions of public and private diplomacy to resolve the crisis virtually blindfolded.[38]

In later describing how the Cuban Missile Crisis had affected his understanding of the main adversary, Khrushchev said in the part of his taped memoirs kept confidential until the end of the Cold War: "Thanks to President Kennedy the United States began to weigh its words more carefully and take into account the Soviet Union's military strength. America began to understand that if it could not be friends with the Soviet Union, at least it should not incite conflict. For us, that was a big victory." He also said—in an acknowledgment of mutual deterrence—that the crisis was a "classic example" of the fact that if both sides "keep military strength at reasonable levels, we should be able to avoid war."[39] In a personal letter to Kennedy after the crisis, he wrote of mutual trust and claimed that there now was "a special relationship" between them.[40] Both Khrushchev and Kennedy, and even more importantly subsequent leaders on both sides throughout the Cold War, showed—if not an appreciation of "reasonable levels" of deterrents—a new, deeper understanding of the need for the adversaries not only not to resort to war in the nuclear age but also to conduct relations in such a way that the risk of war would not be raised. No more bluffing or ultimatums. Khrushchev's behavior in his remaining two years in office also showed an awareness of the need for each side to "weigh its words more carefully and take into account" the other side's military strength and "not incite conflict." Both his assessment of the main adversary and his recognition of the need for prudence in Soviet policy in dealing with it were importantly affected by the chastening experience of the crisis.

Following the Cuban Missile Crisis, the two adversaries sought to lessen tensions and reach agreements. President Kennedy took the initiative in breaking the ice with a major speech, "Toward a Strategy of Peace," on June 10, 1963, that set a new tone for US-Soviet relations. Kennedy called upon Americans to "reexamine our attitude toward the Soviet Union" and—in a reference to the importance of perceptions—"not to fall into the same trap as the Soviets, not to see only a distorted and desperate view of the other side, not to see conflict as inevitable, accommodation as impossible, and communication as nothing more than an exchange of threats." He even urged that Americans "reexamine our attitude to the cold war," calling for a "strategy of peace" and declaring that "we can seek a relaxation of tensions without relaxing our guard." Specifically he called for agreement on a direct communication link between Washington and Moscow and on a nuclear test ban.[41] Khrushchev told his advisers, and later Ambassador Harriman, that the speech was the best by an American president since Roosevelt, and years later senior Soviet diplomats told me the speech had had a great impact in Moscow. It serves as an example of the importance of leadership statements in affecting an adversary's understanding.

Khrushchev responded favorably less than a month later, and a ban on all nuclear tests except underground ones was reached before the end of July.[42] Agreements were also rapidly concluded on a bilateral "hotline" for crisis communications and on not placing nuclear weapons in outer space.[43] These agreements constituted significant opening steps toward lessening tensions, and both Khrushchev and Kennedy seemed ready to move further despite remaining doubts and opposition in both countries. Then Kennedy's assassination changed the political landscape. Khrushchev believed the act resulted from a conspiracy of right-wing American militarists and Texas oil barons and carried ominous implications for US policy.[44] He and his colleagues considered how best to establish relations with Kennedy's successor, but before Lyndon Johnson's election as president in his own right, Khrushchev was ousted.

CHAPTER THREE

Brezhnev
Engagement and Détente, 1965–79

Leonid Brezhnev was first among equals in the collective leadership that dismissed and replaced Khrushchev in October 1964. At Communist Party congresses in 1966 and 1971, they adopted as their general foreign policy line: War must be avoided, peaceful coexistence must prevail, and there should be détente between the capitalist and socialist countries.[1] They stepped up arms programs, however, because they rejected Khrushchev's substitution of bluster for military spending as a path to the kind of equality that the United States would acknowledge and take into account. They accepted the case made by the military establishment and military-industrial complex—which had not fared well under Khrushchev—for expanded Soviet military programs.[2] These included building up forces in the Far East to counter China as well as to provide a better deterrent vis-à-vis the main adversary. Also, Brezhnev, who sometimes wore a medal-encrusted military uniform (he promoted himself to the rank of marshal of the Soviet Union in 1976), chaired the increasingly important Defense Council, where he used allies such as Dmitry Ustinov, head of the Defense Industry Department of the Central Committee, and Marshal Andrei Grechko, the minister of defense (and wartime comrade of Brezhnev's), to bolster his leadership position.

The increase in military spending and forces was not sudden or sharp, but it was sustained because it rested on persistent institutional advocacy as well as perceived requirements. It was also fed by the dynamics of competition with the American buildup. Intelligence on American military programs, with a bias for exaggeration, was one important source of support for further Soviet buildup. In contrast to Khrushchev's interventions, the political leadership in the Brezhnev era made no attempt to moderate or even to monitor the sustained military buildup. Although his policies contributed to an arms race, Brezhnev eschewed Khrushchev's saber-rattling and attempts at coercive diplomacy. Moreover, despite his own rather unsophisticated understanding of foreign policy, his policies did not preclude the development of better-informed understanding of international affairs and of the United States in governing circles.

Political leaders and other Soviet officials, who were developing a greater appreciation of the realities of world politics, hoped that increased Soviet military strength would engender greater acceptance of Soviet political influence in the world. For that goal, more interaction with the West was necessary, and Brezhnev led the way in developing détente first with Western Europe and then with the United States. America thus became a partner as well as an adversary, blurring the image of the enemy. Ideologically there was no change in the traditional view of a rising socialist world pitted against a historically doomed but still powerful capitalist world, but in practice détente with America became the path to gaining respect and acknowledgment by the main adversary that the USSR had in fact "arrived" as an equal superpower.

Focusing on their internal problems and not facing any immediate foreign policy challenges, the new Soviet leaders were inclined to take a cautious and even passive role in international affairs. They were therefore guardedly receptive when the recently elected President Lyndon Johnson in January 1965 sought to arrange a summit meeting. They entered into planning for such a meeting, but they decided the time was not propitious to sit down with an American president who was escalating intervention in the war in Vietnam. A tentatively planned summit was therefore set aside.[3]

Détente meant, of course, a relaxation of tensions but between two sides that remained counterposed in a systemic confrontation. Thus geopolitical competition continued, and a return to greater tensions and even war remained possibilities despite improved US-Soviet relations and formal agreements. The wartime generation's adjustment of ideological assumptions to greater realism in the 1960s and adoption of cooperative measures to lower the risk of war in the 1970s affected the thinking of many officials in the postwar generation. To be sure, this development of a more realistic and enlightened understanding of the world was cautious and limited, and—unsurprisingly in light of the contradictions implicit in détente between ideological opposites—there remained countercurrents and setbacks. The change nonetheless came to shape the views of many officials, advisers, and academics serving in virtually all official and policy-related institutions dealing with foreign affairs. Some of these individuals would play important roles in the final phase of the Cold War.

To support this new policy, Soviet leaders took steps in the late 1960s to improve their understanding of, and to influence, the main adversary. In 1967 an Institute of the USA was established in the Academy of Sciences to cultivate influential Americans—a form of high-level academic propaganda—and, more important, to deepen Soviet knowledge about and ability to deal with the main adversary. Its head, Academician Georgy Arbatov, who had worked at the Institute of the World Economy and International Relations (IMEMO) and served as a member of a key group of consultants to party secretary Yury Andropov, had never met an American. In his memoir Arbatov disclosed that the first major report prepared by his new institute, submitted to the leadership in April 1968, was a secret study that concluded the United States had serious internal economic problems, that the next president might therefore seek better relations with the Soviet Union, and that the Soviet side could help bring this about. This assessment was bolder than any advanced by Soviet diplomats or intelligence analysts, but Arbatov believed that the institute should raise such viewpoints even if they were controversial or unwelcome to some leaders.[4]

Also in 1967, Brezhnev's appointment of Andropov as chairman of the KGB led to some improvement in intelligence analysis. Early on, Andropov requested a major KGB assessment of US policy and found it could not produce—even when allowed three or four months—the kind of report he wanted both to inform the political leadership and to invigorate the entire intelligence service.[5] The KGB's First Chief Directorate (PGU), as the foreign intelligence service was called, had by this time—two decades into the Cold War—developed its competence in espionage and covert action. Its headquarters in Moscow had evolved from a staff of only 120 in 1939, up to 248 when the USSR entered the war in 1941, down to 135 in 1942, 197 in 1943, then up to 600 in 1946, to about 3,000 by the mid-1960s, to about 12,000 in the mid-1980s, and to its peak of about 20,000 in the second half of the 1980s.[6] Its analytical capability had not grown commensurately, however, leaving Soviet leaders to rely on the Foreign Ministry, Party Central Committee staff, and the Ministry of Defense as well as academic experts, consultants, other advisers, and not least on themselves to evaluate important issues. Andropov's arrival helped to relieve the intelligence analysts from their internal reputation as a backwater for "burned" (exposed) and burned-out officers and give them a more respected status and role, albeit still subject to constraints imposed by ideological and politico-bureaucratic considerations.

Andropov's appointments in 1973 of Vladimir Kryuchkov from the Central Committee staff as head of the PGU (until 1988) and of Col. (soon made major general) Nikolai Leonov as head of the PGU's Information-Analytical Department (until 1984) led to further improvements in Soviet intelligence analysis, particularly on the main adversary. They raised the standards, prestige, and career progression associated with analysis. Andropov stressed brevity in reports and initiated a daily intelligence digest, and Leonov raised both competence and morale among analysts although he was unable to persuade Andropov and Kryuchkov to build his department up as much he believed was needed. Leonov bemoans that while CIA had a roughly 1:1 ratio of analysts to operations officers, the KGB in the 1970s and 1980s had a comparable ratio of only about 1:10. Leonov does not state the number of personnel in the Information-Analytical Department; former KGB colonel Oleg Gordievsky has estimated it to have expanded from fewer than seventy in the mid-1970s to more than five hundred by the mid-1980s.[7]

Kryuchkov recruited intelligence officers from graduates of Moscow State University, the Institute of International Relations, the Military-Political Institute, and the Institute of Foreign Languages (and sent junior KGB officers to such schools), and in the KGB's own Intelligence School he instituted a new department for training in analytical work. The KGB increased contacts with the heads of the main civilian Academy of Sciences institutes—Arbatov at the USA and Canada Institute (Canada was added to its scope in 1974) and Nikolai Inozemtsev and later Yevgeny Primakov at IMEMO. Andropov also established a "Group of Consultants to the Chief of the KGB" to advise him on improving analysis (including Arbatov and probably Primakov).

Leonov's headquarters analysts felt free to caution against or disregard KGB political reporting from the field, which was often quite poor. The New York residency, for example, made errors in the names and ranks of UN diplomats, showed lack of understanding of American and world political issues, and quoted Communist Party USA (CPUSA) sources as authoritative commentators on the American scene. Leonov is proud of what he describes as greater freedom to debate issues in his department, where he introduced brainstorming sessions, and some of his analysts developed a less ideologically deformed understanding of the main adversary as data about the West poured into the Center. They were, however, mindful of the biases of Leonov himself, Kryuchkov, and Andropov, and the views they expressed tended to be more hostile toward the United States than the attitudes of the political leaders they served.[8] Moreover, although analysis was often constructive and useful, it also provided a vehicle for erroneous interpretation distorted by ideological and other biases.

As détente with the United States advanced despite America's playing of the China card and continued engagement in a war against North Vietnam, KGB leaders worried that both the political leaders whom they served and the analysts who worked for them were not properly assessing the main adversary. One important development in the relationship between the Soviet Union and the United States, with important implications for Soviet understanding of the main adversary, was the sharp deterioration in Soviet relations with China after 1969 and the not unrelated remarkable improvement in American relations with China after 1971.

Sino-Soviet relations had always included elements of potential and sometimes actual friction, but by 1960 they had deteriorated into a competitive ideological and political relationship within the international communist movement and in bilateral state relations. One contributing element was Chinese criticism of Soviet relations with the United States, expressed most directly when Khrushchev had visited China soon after his visit to the United States in 1959. These polemical criticisms of Soviet policy after even the guarded and limited improvement in Soviet-American relations in 1959, restored in 1963 after the interim Soviet-American crises over Berlin and Cuba, had been aimed in part at Khrushchev's erratic foreign policy course. Khrushchev's successors, hoping to restore better ties with China after his downfall, soon discovered that the Chinese quarrel was not only with the mercurial Khrushchev but with the consistent and continuing Soviet endorsement of "peaceful coexistence" in the contest with the imperialist camp. Moreover, long-standing Chinese resentment over Russian territorial expansion into areas once under Chinese rule reasserted itself, at first in semiofficial polemics against "the new tsars" but by early 1969 in armed incursions into still-disputed border areas.

The worsening of Sino-Soviet relations not only led to a substantial Soviet military buildup and observable military exercises testing possible air attacks on China but also to discreet unofficial probing of the probable American reaction to a possible Soviet strike on Chinese nuclear facilities. Publicly Undersecretary of State Elliot Richardson expressed American concern over any "escalation of this quarrel into a massive breach of international peace and security." And Ambassador Anatoly Dobrynin advised Moscow that the United States would not remain passive and there would be risk of a serious US-Soviet confrontation. KGB intelligence analysts were divided, as were other Soviet officials. The idea of an attack, if ever seriously contemplated by the leaders (as it was at least by some in the military), was shelved. There is some evidence that the Soviet action represented a disinformation campaign to place pressure on the Chinese, in which case it backfired, as one consequence was to contribute to the Chinese decision to improve relations with the United States.[9]

During the early 1970s, Soviet relations with China had reached such a serious state of confrontation (Soviet intelligence on China was poor despite intense efforts) that some intelligence officers even proposed that China rather than the United States should be considered the main adversary. After considerable discussion, it was decided that China should be regarded as a "major" adversary but not the "main" adversary.[10]

KGB (and other international affairs) analysts in Moscow had been divided on whether there was serious possibility of a US-China alliance against the Soviet Union or whether (as most believed) the United States and China would remain competitive, if not hostile.[11] The sudden secret trip by Henry Kissinger to Beijing in July 1971 and the formal visit by President Nixon in February 1972 shocked the Soviet leadership. Gromyko was greatly distressed, even before Brezhnev dressed him down for not foreseeing it.[12]

The Sino-Soviet conflict contributed to "triangular diplomacy" and bolstered both Chinese and American positions countering Soviet interests. It also contributed indirectly to Soviet détente with the West, both for geopolitical reasons (the Soviet Union seeking a more calm western front while facing a Chinese challenge in the east) and indirectly as a consequence of Soviet ideological conflict and confrontation with China. To emphasize the Soviet ideological position versus the apparent Chinese readiness to challenge Soviet and Western interests in a bellicose manner, the Soviets firmed up and emphasized their dedication to peaceful coexistence and the need to avoid war and the risk of war in policy actions as well as in ideological and political rhetoric.[13]

Both the Soviet Union and China supported North Vietnam against the United States during the war in Vietnam (from 1964 to 1973) but competitively rather than jointly and with the United States dealing separately with each on the issue. The Vietnam War was an important obstacle to improving US-Soviet relations, but when it came to a critical juncture on the eve of the first US-Soviet summit meeting in June 1972, the Soviet leaders decided (despite sharp differences among them) to proceed with the meeting despite an American intensification of bombing Hanoi virtually on the eve of the summit.[14]

In his memoir, General Leonov states that his analysis department had to wage a constant battle against "illusions of détente with the United States."[15] In the early 1970s Andropov developed "Theses of a Soviet Intelligence Doctrine for the 1970s," stating that the main task of intelligence was to learn enemy military strategic plans and warnings to prevent a surprise nuclear missile attack on the Soviet Union.[16] In contrast, in 1968, in his first annual report to Brezhnev as KGB chairman, Andropov had stated that the first priority of KGB intelligence collection was political, not military, information, writing that "the intelligence services of the KGB attributed primary significance to the timely acquisition of secret information on subversive plots of the enemy." The report had not contained a word even about the possibility of a surprise American attack.[17] Again in late 1974, when détente was faltering, Andropov exhibited special hostility toward America by railing in a speech against Western reactionaries for sabotaging Soviet peace overtures, suggesting indirectly that the overtures had been rebuffed and had not served as stepping-stones leading to improved relations.[18]

Andropov was not above suppressing or distorting KGB information. For example, Maj. Gen. Oleg Kalugin has revealed that the Washington residency, relying on good sources at a time when he headed its political reporting, told the Center that the CIA had *not* acted to destabilize Czechoslovakia before the Soviet military intervention in 1968. Andropov chose not to pass this information to the Politburo since it contradicted his bias and the Soviet propaganda line. (The KGB was, in fact, then buttressing official propaganda by fabricating evidence of American plotting, including planting caches of US-produced small arms to be "discovered" and identified as a US contribution to a Czech uprising.)[19]

On the rare occasions when senior KGB officers expressed opinions that were inconsistent with customary depictions of America, their comments were ignored. In June 1978 the KGB's *rezident* in Washington (Maj. Gen. Dmitry Yakushkin, who later headed the PGU's USA and Canada Department) expressed a personal evaluation that Americans would never accept what they regarded as a still "backward" Russia as a strategic power equivalent to the United States but rather would "do all they can to weaken their main adversary and *cease living in permanent fear*." This was a striking departure from the standard judgment that the United States was seeking world domination rather than being driven by genuine concern over Soviet capability to destroy the United States. The year 1978 was of course a time of American concerns over an alleged "window of vulnerability," a recent "Team B" alternative harder-line intelligence assessment predicting a mounting Soviet threat to build up for an attack on the United States, and the like. Yakushkin did not, however, argue that the United States would strive to retain or regain a decisive military superiority. Instead he argued that "now the Americans are especially determined to follow the internal situation in the Soviet Union because they have concluded that our country is going to enter a crisis period in our development" in three spheres: economic stagnation, nationalistic friction and separatism, and internal political dissidence. In reporting this analysis years later after the end of the Cold War, Lt. Gen. Vadim Kirpichenko, a senior colleague in the PGU to whom Yakushkin had given this evaluation, acknowledged that he did not recognize its significance at the time but had later come to see its validity.[20] General Kirpichenko passed this evaluation on to PGU chief Kryuchkov, but there was no follow-up. Such an evaluation did not of course fit Kryuchkov's or Andropov's image of the main adversary at that time, although Andropov did have growing concerns of his own about the worsening turn of economic and other developments in the Soviet Union about which he wrote many reports to Brezhnev from the mid-1970s on—which Brezhnev simply noted and consigned to the files.[21]

Military intelligence targeted the main adversary using a sizable share of its communications interception capability, attaché corps, and espionage network (which included some of the most important agents in the United States). Its analytical work was heavily weighted toward assessing the military strengths of potential enemies, especially the United States, and was prone to exaggeration, not because of lack of data but owing to a desire to make military estimates "useful" to the military-industrial complex. For example, as part of an effort to assess major-weapon production potential, the GRU in 1974 estimated that the United States could in wartime produce annually 70,000 tanks, including 50,000 main battle tanks (an absurd total).[22] More than a decade later, when GRU analysts told Chief of the General Staff Marshal Sergei Akhromeyev they wanted to reduce the estimate to (a still greatly exaggerated) 28,500 main battle tanks per year, he demanded that instead that the original number be *raised* "by 25,000," thus boosting the official estimate arbitrarily to 75,000 (a realistic estimate would have been 500). Clearly the "right" answer was not the best estimate but the one that best justified maintaining and modernizing the huge *Soviet* tank inventory.[23]

Our focus in this analysis is not on intelligence operations such as espionage or clandestine political measures, but several aspects of the East-West "intelligence war" bear mention for their impact on Soviet views. General Kirpichenko tells us in his memoir, "The context of the term 'the main adversary' in our operational lexicon over the course of time has undergone changes, but at all times we meant by it above all the special [intelligence] services of the USA."[24] As détente with America was at its height, the KGB residency in Washington increased from about 120 officers in 1970 to about 220 in 1975.[25] In 1974 Kryuchkov established in the First Department (USA) of the PGU a special staff called "Group North," supervised by Kirpichenko, to coordinate espionage and other intelligence activities against American targets outside the United States. KGB residencies in most Western and some Third World countries also set up "main adversary groups" to organize efforts against American targets and interests, although it appears this task was often treated as simply generating reports to meet a bureaucratic tasking requirement.[26]

Another consequence of the intelligence war was that the intense competition with the other side's intelligence services led Soviet intelligence officers to credit the American intelligence services with many US policies they deemed harmful to the USSR. Writing in his post–Cold War memoir, Lt. Gen. Leonid Shebarshin, head of the KGB's foreign intelligence service, the PGU, from 1988 through 1991, still saw the CIA as having been "the driving force" of the Cold War.[27]

The KGB's conduct of deception, disinformation, and propaganda operations around the world usually had the main adversary as its principal target.[28] This led to a tendency for KGB officers to seek out information that would assist missions such as acquiring genuine secret American documents that could be transformed with forged passages and used secretly in influencing third countries or publicly as black propaganda. "Active measures" sometimes also had blowback impact as Soviet diplomats, officials, or GRU officers reported back to Moscow information about the United States they had collected from contacts to whom KGB officers had fed Soviet disinformation.

Perhaps the most important observation related to intelligence operations is that Soviet espionage was not able to produce the most valuable kind of information: high-level information on the adversary's thinking, intentions, and plans. Efforts to improve espionage against the United States had produced successful penetrations of the US military (while most were at low levels, they included individuals with access to top-secret military documents and codes) and information on secret scientific/technical developments (especially concerning weapons and technology). Soviet (and American) espionage was also heavily invested in operations against the intelligence services of the other side. Not only were many successful penetrations members of the opponent's intelligence services, but most were also the result of initiative by the defector or "defector in place" rather than of recruitment. Also, the great majority were owing to greed or personal problems rather than political or ideological disaffection.

Except for reports about high-level NATO alliance coordination, Soviet intelligence was unable to supply valid policy-relevant information as valuable as that obtained by the leaders and their closest policy advisers in increasing interactions directly with American and other Western leaders and officials. Although some three to four hundred pages of intelligence reporting and analysis were sent daily to the leadership (mostly via the Central Committee General Department, headed by Konstantin Chernenko), Soviet leaders including Brezhnev received only the small fraction their personal staffs thought worth bringing to their attention, and its influence seems not to have been substantial.

In addition to being subject to the anti-American bias of Andropov and other senior KGB chiefs, Soviet leaders received biased information about the American scene provided by leaders of the CPUSA. These views came via the International Department of the

Party's Central Committee but were sensibly ignored by all but the department's chief, Boris Ponomarev, and senior Politburo member Mikhail Suslov, the leader whose views were most affected by devotion to ideological orthodoxy. The International Department also evaluated political intelligence provided by the KGB and advised the General Department on what intelligence to bring to Brezhnev's attention. Information going to the leaders was subject to bias in selection as well as slanting performed by the intelligence services. For example, Brezhnev was often given exaggerated or fabricated reports on how well his speeches were received by publics around the world, and General Kirpichenko states that pessimistic and unpleasant reports were often kept from Brezhnev in order not to "upset" him.[29] Also, the PGU was usually careful to avoid initiatives or even reporting that implied support for controversial changes in Soviet policy. Such caution further diminished the already limited influence of Soviet intelligence at the top political level. As General Kalugin has summarized the point, "the opinion of Intelligence was usually ignored or not even seen by political leaders deciding most important foreign policy questions."[30]

Foreign Minister Gromyko was prepared to deal with the United States as a partner *because* it was the main adversary. His personal role allowed his ministry to play an important part in Soviet policy decisions relating to the United States in the 1970s and beyond. He created his own brain trust of advisers who, among other things, reviewed and briefed him on the intelligence provided to him by the KGB and GRU.[31] The Foreign Ministry did not produce intelligence evaluations per se, but its policy recommendations often were accompanied by relevant assessments of US affairs. Although not immune from a tendency to tell the leaders what they wanted to hear, Ambassador Dobrynin in Washington offered more frank and informative appraisals of American policies and aims than his predecessors and exercised some influence on Soviet policy.[32]

The blurring of the image of the Western powers as Soviet policy embraced a serious effort to lessen tensions with them in the early

1970s was accompanied by leadership frictions. Brezhnev had consolidated his position as unchallenged leader by 1973 and brought into the Politburo—for the first time since 1953—the key guardians of Soviet national security (Foreign Minister Gromyko, Defense Minister Grechko, and KGB chief Andropov), all of whom supported his détente policy. Clearing the way for a sustained commitment to the policy, unreconstructed cold warriors such as Ukrainian party chief Pyotr Shelest, who had opposed the 1972 Moscow summit with Nixon, were removed from the Politburo in the early to mid-1970s. Even among those who supported détente there remained countercurrents of skepticism regarding the main adversary. Andropov remained ever the skeptic about US aims, and Suslov was leery even of rhetoric that emphasized shared Soviet-American interests or downplayed Soviet support for world communist solidarity. Brezhnev's wartime crony Marshal Grechko weighed in to keep Soviet military strength a key element in the policy, supporting arms control only reluctantly and working until his death in 1976 to ensure that agreed constraints were not far-reaching.[33]

The Soviet campaign for a détente in relations between East and West in Europe was launched by Brezhnev in 1966 at the Twenty-Third Communist Party Congress. In addition to wanting to stabilize the European scene while facing a hostile China in the East, Soviet leaders wanted to neutralize what many in Moscow saw as a possibly resurgent West German threat. But the main purpose was to confront the United States with the need to choose: détente or confrontation. Accordingly in 1966, and continuing until mid-1970, the Soviet and Warsaw Pact advocacy of European security and détente was addressed to the Western Europeans—not to the United States, which was not included in the proposals for European security (and, of course, NATO was similarly excluded).

There had been increasing support for a European détente in Western Europe. President Charles de Gaulle sought to establish an independent French role in Europe, visiting Moscow in 1966 and loosening ties with NATO. In West Germany, the previous hard line against ties with the East began to be dismantled that same year. And even NATO that year commissioned a study of future trends in the alliance, which led to NATO endorsement of détente before the end of 1967. The Soviet-Warsaw Pact intervention in Czechoslovakia in 1968 slowed the movement toward détente in Europe in both the East and the West but only briefly. Some saw it as demonstrating the need for détente.

By 1969, under a new administration in Washington, US-Soviet relations were revivified. President Richard Nixon and his national security adviser, Henry Kissinger, were concerned about the danger of a European détente weakening NATO and excluding the United States from at least some European security arrangements, especially with a new West German government moving more actively on its own *Ostpolitik*. So the United States began to be more supportive. And in June 1970 the Warsaw Pact explicitly changed its proposals to include the United States and Canada in a European security conference.

The Soviet leaders had probably sought a comprehensive East-West détente as their preferred outcome from the outset but were of course prepared as a fallback, if the United States remained opposed, to use détente in Europe to weaken or divide the Western alliance. A Soviet-West German agreement also quickly followed in 1970, and in 1971 an agreement was finally reached on Berlin.

Hence by the time of the first Soviet-American summit meeting in Moscow in June 1972, agreement was reached on both a Soviet-American détente relationship featuring strategic arms limitations by the two powers and concrete steps to hold a European security conference (in Helsinki in 1975) and to open negotiations on mutual and balanced force reductions (MBFR) in Central Europe by countries of NATO and the Warsaw Pact.[34]

The Soviet leaders by 1972 had decided that a security relationship between the Soviet Union and its Warsaw Pact allies with the main adversary and its NATO allies was in their interest and that there was a mutual interest shared by adversaries. This was very important politically, in terms of mutual security, and as a major modification of the traditional Soviet understanding of the main adversary and of the general adversarial relationship of socialist and capitalist states. The United States remained the main adversary, but the context of the relationship had significantly changed.

This change had not come easily. A number of Soviet leaders (and still more at lower levels of the party and government bureaucracies) had opposed or at least not shared the new General Line (as the official policy line was known). Long after the defeat and retirement of Stalinists such as Molotov, Kaganovich, and Voroshilov came the departure from the Politburo of new hard-liners and unreconstructed cold warriors of the next generation, such as Shelest (ousted in 1972 after opposing the first Brezhnev-Nixon summit), Voronov (1973), former party secretary (and for a time KGB chief) Shelepin (1975), and titular president Podgorny (1977). New members of the Politburo in 1973, with a policy of détente with the adversary clearly established, as earlier noted included the heads of the key national security organizations: Foreign Minister Andrei Gromyko, Defense Minister Marshal Andrei Grechko (succeeded after his death in 1976 by Dmitry Ustinov), and KGB chairman Yury Andropov. Brezhnev by then was the unchallenged leader.[35]

Throughout the 1970s, the "decade of détente," there remained differences of view on various détente policies among Soviet leaders (as among members of the American administrations). Marshal Grechko, for example, was a very reluctant supporter of arms control negotiations with the United States, and his conservative stance helped ensure that agreements reached were generally not far-reaching in real constraints. Mikhail Suslov, for his part, was leery of policies or even rhetoric that downplayed Soviet support for world communist solidarity and emphasized shared Soviet-American aims and actions. (This was, of course, not unlike parallel differences of view on the American side.) These differences were also reflected in programmatic declarations and concrete programs and in policies toward Western Europe and the Third World.

There was, however, general agreement that the very fact of the Soviet-American bilateral summit meetings (five in the 1970s), as well as joint declarations calling for and reflecting parity and equality of the two superpowers, represented a significant gain for the Soviet Union. In Soviet terms, this reflected a favorable shift in the "correlation of forces" between the two sides to a rough balance, overcoming finally the traditional Soviet weakness that Khrushchev had prematurely tried to boost by bluff. Similarly, the fruits of détente in Europe, above all the successful conclusion of the Conference on Security and Cooperation in Europe (CSCE) in Helsinki in 1975, were seen as a great achievement of Soviet diplomacy in confirming and stabilizing the postwar territorial and other restructuring of Europe, including implicit acceptance of the East-West division of the continent. (Again, a counterpart was conservative American criticism of President Gerald Ford for agreeing to the Helsinki CSCE Accord.) In the long run, of course, détente in Europe and the Helsinki Accord in particular proved to be an important step in leading to the end of the Cold War and the emergence of an undivided Europe.

Brezhnev, secure in power but with deteriorating health and competence by the late 1970s, throughout the decade had held to a course of détente that included a shared role with the United States, despite his worldview based on the traditional Soviet ideological postulation of the inevitable historical rise of socialism and decline of capitalism in the world. Unlike Khrushchev, he did not seek to jump-start history and regarded the United States as an historical adversary but not necessarily—and preferably not—adversarial in all respects. Of course he sought to protect and advance Soviet interests, but he did not assume that precluded even significant areas of common action with the United States and avoidance of risks of war. His approach was not inconsistent with that taken by his American counterparts Nixon, Kissinger, Ford, and Jimmy Carter (when pursuing Cyrus Vance's policy line, although decreasingly as Carter came to pursue the more aggressively competitive policies of Zbigniew Brzezinski).

The Soviet-American détente of 1972–79 moderated, but did not replace or supplant, the reciprocal perceptions of opposing adversaries. In the popular images (on both sides), the other side was seen and depicted as departing from détente in numerous ways when policies and actions collided. The leaders, on both sides, were sometimes surprised and often troubled by many actions of the other side. But the Soviet (and American) leaders did not ever believe that détente had meant that the adversarial relationship had been banished. The main problem was that leaders on *both* sides believed that détente should mean that the other side would moderate its behavior but that its own pursuit of advantage should be acceptable. Leaders on both sides saw advantage in negotiated agreements to curb some extremes of the strategic arms race, but "prudence" (and the powerful political weight of those with vested interests in the military-industrial complexes of the two sides as well as the professional military leaders) limited the scope of agreements. On the other hand, agreements such as measures to avert naval incidents at sea, like the earlier hot-line communication link (now upgraded), were seen as based on reciprocal and shared interests. There were, to be sure, problems in some cases when leaders could not carry out their commitments and agreements—most notably and seriously when Presidents Nixon and Ford could not obtain necessary congressional action to permit delivery of promised trade arrangements. Moreover, public opinion in the United States shifted from strong initial support for détente to more skeptical questioning under the arguments of opponents of détente by the mid-1970s. In 1976, an election year, President Ford even dropped use of the word "détente" as he was challenged by opponents in his own party. But on the whole, the chief problem was that leaders on both sides continued to pursue diplomatic and other courses of action that were seen to serve their own national interests, without much regard for the interests and concerns of the other side.

As noted, Brezhnev and his colleagues believed the correlation of forces had shifted in their favor, making the Soviet Union a second global superpower on a par with its main adversary. Thus, in their view, US presidents had improved American relations with the USSR because they were compelled by their recognition of changed objective reality to turn to a cooperative regulation of the continuing historical contest between the two world systems. A Politburo and government statement at the time of the 1972 Brezhnev-Nixon summit ascribed "great international significance" to the signed agreement on "Basic Principles of Relations between the United States and the USSR" precisely because it was seen in Moscow as registering this recognition.[36] A secret Central Committee letter to senior Communist Party officials went beyond the public commentary, stating that "the very fact that Nixon *had to sign* a document that speaks of both sides placing the principle of peaceful coexistence at the basis of their relations" reflected "an important change in the correlation of forces" and "bears witness to a strong moral-political victory for the Soviet Union, and a weakening of the position of American imperialism."[37]

Soviet leaders thus saw Brezhnev's summits with US presidents in the early 1970s as marking an important advance in Soviet power and prestige. Similarly, the fruits of détente in Europe, above all the successful conclusion of the Conference on Security and Cooperation in Europe (CSCE) in Helsinki in 1975, were seen at the time as a signal achievement of Soviet diplomacy in stabilizing the postwar restructuring of Europe, including implicit acceptance of its East-West division.[38] These perceived successes did not lead Soviet leaders to believe that the historically determined adversarial relationship between the USSR and the United States had ended, but they did create an expectation that America would moderate its international behavior while accepting prudent pursuit by the USSR of its own advantage. American perceptions mirrored this Soviet view, assuring future difficulties as leaders on both sides pursued courses of action with little regard for the other side's concerns and with undue expectations that their own actions would be acquiesced in by their adversary.

Political leaders on both sides of the Cold War were inclined to reach their own conclusions about their counterparts. Most members of the Soviet leadership right down into the 1980s continued to be influenced by such stereotypes as belief that monopoly capitalists really ran the US government behind the scenes and could not comprehend that presidents such as Richard Nixon could not make decisions that Congress would not support. As Ambassador Dobrynin has remarked, the understanding of the United States (and foreign affairs in general) of most Politburo members was essentially limited to what they read in *Pravda*.[39] Personal contact of the principal Soviet leaders with American presidents was always a key factor in Soviet policymaking, especially when the leader was in a strong political position (Stalin until his death in 1953, Khrushchev from 1958 to 1963, and Brezhnev from 1973 to 1980). Moreover, the position taken by the leader (except in time of shared leadership or transition) usually precluded serious deliberation of issues.

CHAPTER FOUR

Brezhnev, Andropov
Tensions Revived, 1979–84

East-West détente peaked in 1975, following Brezhnev's summits with Presidents Nixon and Ford in the early 1970s and the CSCE Accord that year in Helsinki.[1] The next ten years saw a decline in Soviet relations with the United States brought on by a series of events culminating in 1983 when tensions caused Soviet leaders to view the USSR's main adversary with alarm, wondering even whether America was preparing for military confrontation. A final Brezhnev summit with an American president and the signing of another major strategic arms limitation agreement in 1979 could not stop the downward trend, which greatly accelerated after Soviet military forces invaded Afghanistan late in 1979 and Ronald Reagan became president in early 1981.

One factor in the downturn was the USSR's decision to involve itself more actively in support of national liberation movements and civil wars in the Third World. Soviet leaders allowed ideologically stimulated hopes for a wave of progressive, loosely socialist, and anti-Western movements to guide this element of their policy, thinking that strategic nuclear parity with the main adversary gave them room to support those movements in prudent, limited ways short of direct intervention and might also restrain American countermoves. The KGB was generally skeptical of these involvements, but its views were neither sought nor, when cautiously advanced, given attention.[2]

Soviet leaders were dismayed by Washington's playing of the China card in 1978–80, as the United States abandoned a policy of equidistance and balance in relations with the Soviet Union and communist China for a distinct "tilt" in favor of relations with China, to the detriment of Soviet interests in relations with the United States, China, and the global balance of power.[3] Central Committee official Valentin Falin stated in 1980: "There is no doubt that China played an important part in the unfavorable turn of United States policy. China, as the White House expected, offered the United States a chance to change the correlation of forces." Similarly, a senior Soviet diplomat told me at the time that while China would not be a real military threat to the Soviet Union for many years, to Moscow the most seriously disturbing element was that the Sino-American rapprochement put the *United States* and its aims in a different light.[4]

The year 1979 and those that followed brought blows to détente that affected Soviet perceptions of the main adversary. That year saw the fifth US-Soviet summit of the decade, a meeting in Vienna in June between Brezhnev and President Jimmy Carter. At the summit, Brezhnev noted that the Soviet leaders were careful not to categorize the United States as an "enemy" or "adversary" and asked for reciprocal treatment from American leaders. Carter, apparently caught off guard, did not comment or reply.[5]

Also soon following the Vienna summit, a political hornets' nest erupted in Washington about intelligence reportedly "finding" a Soviet Army "combat brigade" in Cuba, raising suspicions in Moscow that some in the American leadership had contrived a crisis to undermine the strategic arms limitation treaty agreed to at Vienna.[6] Indeed, the United States did not ratify the treaty, and Soviet leaders wondered whether Carter himself was responsible.[7] Brezhnev declared that he believed the failure to obtain ratification was "not without connivance of Government circles in the United States," that is, in the administration.[8]

In October 1979 the first volume of Henry Kissinger's memoirs (*White House Years*) was published, and in it Kissinger disclosed that

Nixon and he had had a cynical attitude during the heyday of détente. Although practiced themselves in self-serving and hypocritical
postures, the Soviet leaders had been sincere in détente as they con-
ceived it and were disenchanted to learn of the American deceit by
leaders with whom they had personally dealt multiple times and dismayed to find themselves open to potential charges of having been
hoodwinked. Valentin Falin, in the 1970s first deputy chief of the
International Information Department of the Central Committee,
told me years later that Brezhnev had been "shocked" and that the
"unmasking" of the American leadership by one of its central figures
had in the 1980s given ammunition to opponents of détente, who
held that Brezhnev and Gromyko had made a serious error in trusting US interest in détente. I was also told of this impact of the Kissinger memoir on other occasions by Georgy Arbatov and Georgy
Kornienko.[9]

Soviet leaders saw NATO's decision in December 1979 to deploy
advanced Pershing II ballistic and ground-launched cruise missiles
in Western Europe as threatening the strategic balance by enhancing the US capability for launching a sudden nuclear attack on the
Soviet Union. In particular they believed the Pershing II missiles had
the range, accuracy, and short flight time to strike key Soviet strategic and political command centers in the Moscow area.[10] The KGB
and (especially) the GRU provided strong evidence that the missiles
had such capabilities, and their analyses ascribed dire motivations
to US leaders. Moscow's failure to prevent the missile deployments
through propaganda in Western Europe maintained the concern the
aging Soviet leaders felt about Western motivations, which increasingly were even thought to include possible preparation for war.

In 1979 PGU chief Kryuchkov had opposed the idea of Soviet
military intervention in Afghanistan, as did all key military leaders
and some (but not all) military and KGB officers involved in Af-
ghan affairs.[11] But KGB chief Andropov joined Brezhnev, Ustinov,
and Gromyko on December 12 in making the fateful decision. General Leonov has made clear that neither he nor anyone else in the

Information-Analytical Department of the PGU knew anything in advance about the move (and he would have opposed it). The GRU was not informed or asked for an assessment, and no Foreign Ministry official except Gromyko was aware.[12] As had occurred before, no advance assessment of the impact on the main adversary was made, although Gromyko knew it would harm US-Soviet relations. General Kryuchkov has stated that the KGB and GRU had informed the Soviet leadership of US designs for using the Afghan-Soviet border area to replace US intelligence-collection facilities recently lost in Iran and that the main reason for the intervention was defense of Soviet security interests on the southern border, including the possible influx of extremist Islamic influence.[13] Brezhnev and other Soviet leaders—who had not anticipated the long-lasting negative American response—tried to ride out the unforeseen rough waters with the United States despite virtual American abandonment of détente, a stance soon reinforced by the election of Ronald Reagan as president.[14]

Détente collapsed when leaders adopted policies they regarded as necessary or advantageous despite the other side's perceptions of those policies as hostile and directed against its interests or security. Thus Soviet leaders regarded the US rallying of NATO on deployment of new missiles capable of striking key strategic targets in the Soviet Union without warning as a deliberate and dangerous tipping of the strategic balance that provided the foundation for détente. Similarly American leaders regarded the Soviet military intervention in Afghanistan as a dangerous extension of the "Brezhnev Doctrine" beyond the boundaries of the recognized Soviet alliance system and as the first step in a new Soviet offensive into Southwest Asia. These evaluations of the motivations of the other side were seriously off the mark. They indicated, however, how much the situation prevailing only a few years earlier had deteriorated and how enduring images of the main adversary had remained in the minds of leaders on both sides even under détente. Thus, even without a direct clash between the two superpowers, each saw actions by the other that it regarded as hostile and dangerous to its security interests. While these concerns were in most cases exaggerated or misplaced, each did see the other carrying out actions that bore adversely on its interests despite détente undertakings to avoid such practices and that also contained the seeds of possible direct confrontation.

Reagan's disdain for arms control and his determination to intensify a US arms buildup fed enduring images of the main adversary that still persisted in the minds of Soviet leaders and caused some officials to see him as an anti-Soviet cold warrior or even an erratic gunslinger. Nonetheless, the foreign policy line enunciated at the Twenty-Sixth Communist Party Congress in February and March 1981 made a renewed plea for dialogue and détente while castigating the United States for pressing a course of "undermining détente, boosting the arms race, a policy of threats."[15]

Soviet leaders found their concerns heightened when the United States in 1981 initiated unprecedented and unpublicized provocative American naval and air exercises, some with mock attacks on Soviet borders. In January 1981, in one of his first actions, President Reagan approved a proposal to begin a program of psychological harassment actions against the USSR, including authorization in March of "military probes on the Soviet periphery." In August and September 1981 an armada of eighty-three US, UK, and Norwegian naval ships passed through the Norwegian Sea, and some went beyond into the Barents Sea, north of Russia. By avoiding communication, they succeeded in evading detection until they demonstratively made their presence known, to Soviet consternation and concern.[16]

Now facing an apparently determined American policy of pressure and confrontation, Soviet leaders decided they had to guard against the worst-case possibility—a decision by the main adversary to launch a surprise nuclear attack on the Soviet Union. Sometime between March and May 1981, the Politburo approved a proposal by Andropov and Ustinov to launch a new intelligence program by both the KGB and the GRU to monitor all possible indications of US preparations to launch a sudden nuclear-missile attack on the USSR.[17] While not the most likely contingency, it was certainly the most dangerous one and represented a threat that required vigorous and constant but secret measures to discover if the adversary was embarking on such a course. It is not known whether other members of the Politburo shared Andropov's and Ustinov's concerns over such a dire if improbable contingency—most likely not—but no one would object to a secret and passive precautionary alert, especially in light of what was seen in Moscow as the provocative stance of the superpower adversary. As greater tension between the superpowers inflamed alarmists in the Soviet leadership, intelligence became a means not for allaying their fears but for increasing them.

In May, in an unprecedented appearance at a conference of KGB chiefs, Brezhnev led off by denouncing Reagan's policies, setting the stage for KGB chairman Andropov, who asserted that the new US administration was actively preparing for nuclear war and announced that the Politburo had decided that the KGB and the GRU would cooperate in a worldwide operation to monitor any indications of US and NATO measures for the initiation of a nuclear attack, in particular a surprise missile strike.[18] The PGU was placed in charge of the operation, called Surprise Nuclear-Missile Attack (VRYaN) or Nuclear-Missile Attack (RYaN). In early 1983 it was designated as a long-term project (in KGB parlance a "permanent operational assignment"). KGB *rezidenty* in all NATO capitals and some other countries were required to submit biweekly reports to the Center on any and all indications of possible Western preparations to launch nuclear war. In February 1983 new and more detailed instructions were sent to all *rezidenty* in NATO countries emphasizing the increased danger owing to the forthcoming deployment of Pershing II ballistic missiles capable of striking Moscow-area strategic targets in a matter of minutes.[19]

The Center insistently pressed field operatives to look harder for, and report more fully on, something that did not exist, disproportionately tying up collection assets. At its peak in 1983, more than fifty officers in the Center were dedicated to assessing vast amounts of VRYaN biweekly intelligence reporting, reviewing irrelevant indicators and reaffirming there was nothing worth passing on to their leaders.[20] By 1985 the operation was in decline, and it was finally ended by the last head of the KGB, Vadim Bakatin, and the first head of the PGU's successor organization, the SVR (Foreign Intelligence Service), Yevgeny Primakov, on November 27, 1991, just a month before the Soviet Union ceased to exist.[21]

The intelligence reporting gathered under VRYaN shows repeated instances of exaggeration. There also were other distortions. Reportedly, in one case Soviet intelligence obtained a classified American paper quoting a document of the National Security Council in the early 1980s that outlined possible situations in which the United States might decide to go to war, including loss of Middle East oil sources or a communist coup in Mexico. Because it did not include US initiation of war with the Soviet Union or Warsaw Pact, which Soviet intelligence always held to be a permanent American contingent objective, it was decided (presumably by Andropov) to suppress the entire document and not inform the leadership, thus depriving it of the kind of rarely obtained information about adversary plans that usually is most prized.[22] In another instance the GRU issued an erroneous threat warning stemming from coverage of a US Global Shield military exercise, then covered up its mistake without informing the Politburo (or the KGB) when it became clear that there was no real threat.[23]

Yury Andropov left his post as chairman of the KGB in May 1982 to become a party secretary, and when Brezhnev died in November, Andropov succeeded him. He soon found himself facing the most alarming year in US-Soviet relations since the Cuban Missile Crisis in 1962, as the level of hostile American public polemics intensified in 1983 over the already charged level of 1981–82. Reagan accused the USSR of being "the focus of evil in the world" and guilty of "the aggressive impulses of an evil empire," and he called for a "crusade for freedom" to "triumph over evil." There were allegations of Soviet complicity in the assassination attempt on Pope John Paul II in 1981. CIA director William Casey used the site of Churchill's "Iron Curtain" speech to call for a sustained policy of military assistance to "our friends" in the Third World, and shortly thereafter the United States invaded Grenada. Provocative American naval and air incursions in and near Soviet territory and bases greatly increased in 1981–83. And in 1983 Pershing II and ground-launched cruise missiles began to arrive in Europe. Reagan in March 1983 also announced a Strategic Defense Initiative (known as SDI or "Star Wars") to devise a comprehensive, probably space-based, antimissile defense system to make the United States invulnerable.

Reagan's announcement of his intention to pursue SDI presented a challenge to Soviet intelligence. Was it a real and feasible project? Could the Soviet Union maintain mutual deterrence with the United States if it was implemented? If so, how? Or was the purpose to reassure the American people and make more politically feasible at some point an American attack on the Soviet Union? Or was it a bluff, a scam, a deception and disinformation operation to lead the Soviet Union into greatly increasing its already overburdened defense spending? Or was it a ploy to portray a seeming threat that would be traded in arms control talks for real Soviet concessions? Or was it simply a way to increase the profits of American defense industries?

All of these possibilities, including various combinations of considerations, were raised by Soviet intelligence. The first major directive to Soviet foreign intelligence operations in the West (not issued until February 13, 1985, with an eye to forthcoming arms control talks with the United States in Geneva) raised some of these possibilities in the form of reporting on speculation by Western observers, but the directive sought confirming or disconfirming evidence on them all.[24] (There was not even a mention in the directive about Reagan's personal strong interest in seeing SDI pursued and realized.)

A KGB officer serving in Washington at the time has described how he responded to the directive. He was convinced (as were most

KGB officers) that SDI was a bluff to intimidate the Soviets and force a debilitating burden on the Soviet economy. As he set about trying to find reportable information, by happenstance he attended a public meeting at which a member of Congress (Rep. Robert Dornan) discussed SDI and seemed to express the same view he held. He was then able to report it to Moscow as the view of an influential member of Congress.[25]

Even without such reporting, the senior KGB intelligence chiefs apparently suspected that SDI was a bluff intended, above all, to induce the Soviet Union to waste vast expenditures to counter a notional program. Gen. Viktor Grushko, chief of the counterintelligence directorate and later first deputy chief of the KGB, has referred to the many cases of US disinformation that led the Soviet Union into costly false paths of military technology developments that placed a heavy burden on the Soviet economy, citing SDI as a prime example of an attempt to do so.[26]

In separate one-on-one conversations in 1999, both General Kryuchkov and Marshal Dmitry Yazov told me that they believed SDI had been a bluff and disinformation in an attempt to bleed the Soviet economy. Although it seems clear that the KGB concluded that SDI was a bluff, it may have taken some time in the mid-1980s before it reached that conclusion. Also, although Mikhail Gorbachev accepted the advice of scientists that SDI could in any case be countered by less expensive asymmetrical countermeasures, he did not dismiss the possibility that SDI could have some degree of success.

The Soviet space scientist Roald Sagdeyev (who was among the scientists whose advice on SDI Gorbachev accepted) has been cited by some American supporters of the program as saying that SDI caused the Soviet Union to squander large sums unnecessarily. But he has informed me that was *not* what he had said and that it was not true.

SDI was a genuine defense program designed to conduct research and development of unconventional missile-defense systems with the aim of determining if an effective antimissile defense system was feasible. Its advocates and supporters had varying expectations and interests. It was not merely a device to ratchet up Soviet defense spending. It has, however, become known that there *was* a highly secret disinformation component of the program, manipulating certain SDI development tests to exaggerate successes with the aim of misleading the Soviet Union into massive outlays against unreal threats. Whether Soviet intelligence became aware of this deception component of the program before it became publicly known and acknowledged (in 1993) is not known.[27]

What brought matters to a head with respect to Soviet perceptions of the United States was the downing on August 31, 1983, by Soviet air defenses of KAL 007, a South Korean civilian airliner that had strayed off course over Soviet territory, with the loss of 269 lives. The Soviet air defense chiefs believed the errant aircraft was on a military reconnaissance mission for the United States (which had recently been flying both reconnaissance and psychological warfare flights in the region). As soon as the United States had ascertained that it was a civilian airliner and that it had been shot down by a Soviet interceptor aircraft, Secretary of State George Shultz hastily announced that fact, and President Reagan in a series of statements blamed the Soviets for an "atrocity," an "act of barbarism," a "massacre," a "murder of innocent civilians," a "crime against humanity," and an "inexcusable act of brutality." Both sides, initially depending on incomplete information and later seeking to cast all blame on the other, made misleading and inaccurate statements. The speed and vigor with which the United States denounced the action alarmed Soviet leaders, who were further persuaded of American hostility and suspected that the United States might have deliberately provoked the whole incident, as did Reagan's use of the episode in lobbying successfully for his enlarged defense programs.[28]

On September 28 Andropov issued an unusual formal statement, representing the first definitive and authoritative overall Soviet assessment of Reagan administration policy. US policy, he said, constituted "a serious threat to peace," seeking "a dominating position in the world for the United States of America without regard for the interests of other states or peoples." Describing the incident as "a sophisticated provocation organized by the US special [i.e., intelligence] services" and "extreme adventurism in policy," Andropov made clear that any earlier allowances that the Reagan administration would come around to a recognition of realities could no longer be sustained: "If anyone had any illusions about the possibility of an evolution for the better in the policy of the present American administration, recent events have dispelled them once and for all."[29]

Precisely at this critical juncture, an important phenomenon that plagued both Soviet and American military warning and alerting systems throughout the Cold War occurred. On September 26, 1983, the Soviet military intelligence satellite-surveillance-and-warning system seemed to indicate US launch of intercontinental missiles toward the Soviet Union. A relatively junior Soviet duty officer at the monitoring station (Serpukhov-15), Lt. Col. Stanislav Petrov, correctly evaluated it as a false alarm rather than as evidence of an actual attack. Had he judged differently or simply reported it, some higher-level military commander would have had to decide within minutes to report it as an attack, and someone, possibly well below the top political leadership given the time pressure, could well have started the ultimate great war.[30]

Less than two months later, a NATO military exercise called Able Archer, testing the command-and-communication procedures for the release of nuclear weapons in case of war, led the Center and the GRU under VRYaN to send flash cables to key KGB and GRU posts calling urgently for all information relating to possible US preparations for an imminent nuclear strike on the Soviet Union. After the exercise ended, the specific report that had led to the flash messages was found to have been in error, and inasmuch as the Center did not receive indications of a possible attack, no action was taken by Soviet intelligence to alert top Soviet leaders. This was the closest that VRYaN ever came to reaching such a momentous conclusion.[31]

Mikhail Gorbachev has told me the matter never came to the attention of the Politburo. Georgy Kornienko told me it had not been brought up with the Foreign Ministry, and Marshal Sergei Akhromeyev, then first deputy chief of the General Staff, has said there had been no general military alert. Col. Gen. Ivan Yesin of the Strategic Missile Forces has, however, said that SS-19 and SS-20 components of the Soviet intercontinental missile force were placed on alert.[32]

During the tense moments of late 1983, Andropov was foremost in drawing attention to what he saw as threatening US policies and the danger of war. He has been cited as saying to the Politburo in 1983 that the danger of war was then greater than at any other time since the Cuban Missile Crisis and on another occasion to have stated in a cable to KGB posts worldwide that the danger was the greatest since World War II.[33] Other available KGB-cabled reports from 1983 and early 1984 cite statements by PGU chief General Kryuchkov that "the threat of an outbreak of a nuclear war has reached dangerous proportions" and "is reaching an extremely dangerous point."[34]

I found occasion years later to ask a number of former senior Soviet officials whether they really meant what they had said. In a private conversation in 1999, I asked General Kryuchkov when had he considered the US-Soviet relationship to be most dangerous, and he promptly said 1983 was the most alarming time (he cited SDI and KAL 007 but not Able Archer). When I asked about VRYaN, he downplayed it, saying it was really an intelligence watch, "just in case," rather than reflecting real expectation of an attack, even though it was couched in "sharp terms." I asked if he personally had *ever* believed that the United States would launch a nuclear strike on the Soviet Union, and after a moment's reflection he said that he had not. When I asked if other members of the leadership had ever really expected an attack, he said that he thought not. When I pressed, asking if there had been none, he replied, "Maybe Andropov. He was more fearful of an attack than others."

Maj. Gen. Oleg Kalugin, not himself concerned over a possible Western attack, has argued that Andropov was concerned not only because of all the indications in the early 1980s of American hostility to the Soviet Union but also because he was acutely aware of how far the USSR had fallen behind the West in science and technology. Above all, Andropov believed the United States and its Western allies were working day and night to destroy the Soviet Union, and he saw CIA plots and imperialist intrigues everywhere.[35] A number of former intelligence officers (with some exceptions in the GRU) had not considered VRYaN to be a serious program or a Western attack to be a serious threat.

Just as the growing tensions at the outset of the Cold War in 1946–50 gave rise to overstated rhetoric about the threat of war, when both main adversaries depicted the danger in terms "clearer than the truth" (as Dean Acheson elegantly phrased it), so too were the fears of a threatening war in 1981–83 fanned by VRYaN and other Soviet reactions to American expressions of alarm over an alleged "window of vulnerability" to Soviet attack portrayed by the conservatives on the Committee on the Present Danger and Team B. For example, following on the heels of the KAL 007 incident, on September 21 Vice President George H. W. Bush in a speech in Vienna launched a tirade against Soviet hegemony in Eastern Europe, saying that Soviet violation of the Yalta Accord was "the primary root of East-West tensions today." He then referred to the "brutal murder" of the 269 victims on KAL 007 as not civilized behavior "in the European tradition." From there he went on to argue that Russia was not even really European, not having experienced the Renaissance, the Reformation, and the Enlightenment, while praising the European roots of the United States. This gratuitous challenge to the Soviet Union (and Russia, past and future) was taken as an official US statement. No one among the many highly critical *Western* Europeans, or the angered Soviet leaders, knew that the vice president's remarks had not been designed as an official speech. It had not been cleared with the White House or secretary of state, and officials in the Department of State had tried but failed to get Bush to change the speech. (Bush had his eye on his own political future and wanted to shore up his standing with conservative Republicans who he believed considered him too liberal.) But the Soviet leaders were not disposed to see his remarks as simply reflecting domestic American political considerations and interpreted his statement as indicating that the Reagan administration was pulling out all stops to further a political offensive against the Soviet Union.

In apparent contrast to the intense hostility of the Soviet and American intelligence services, at the very peak of tension in 1983 the KGB took an initiative in approaching the CIA and reaching agreement to create a telephonic hotline to arrange meetings for clarification of potentially dangerous misunderstandings. This contact, called "the Gavrilov channel," allowed direct meetings on and off during the next several years.[36] This remarkable agreement testified to the depth of concern felt by intelligence professionals on both sides—but especially the Soviet side—during this most tense political confrontation during the Cold War. It also demonstrated the ability of the main adversaries, in secrecy and without political posturing, on occasion to seek sensible and mutually useful clarifications aimed at dispelling potentially dangerous misperceptions.

The year 1984 was devoted to a wary exploration of improving relations. President Reagan, when advised (on the basis of Gordievsky's reports to the British) that Able Archer and other things had raised serious alarms in the Soviet leadership over a possible American attack, was incredulous but disquieted and sought to find ways to reassure them. Perhaps spurred also by the launch of his own reelection campaign, he responded positively to a proposal by Secretary Shultz that he make a speech urging renewal of a dialogue with the Soviet Union. Speaking on January 16, 1984, Reagan affirmed the need for "credible deterrence, peaceful competition, and constructive cooperation" to be reached through serious dialogue.[37] The initial Soviet response was a tepid statement that the Soviet Union did not need to be convinced of the need for dialogue since that already was its policy. It also declared that the dialogue must be between equals and that it was "by practical deeds that we will judge whether the United States has serious intentions of conducting a dialogue with us." Issued in Andropov's name, this was the last gasp of the Andropov freeze dating back to September 1983. Two weeks later, on February 9, Andropov died and was succeeded by the colorless, aging, and ailing Konstantin Chernenko—who filled an interregnum for a year before he too died, on March 10, 1985.

Chernenko was not a notable political thinker or strategist, but he had been a faithful supporter of détente under Brezhnev and, as chief of the General Department of the Central Committee, at least nominally had supervised decisions regarding what intelligence should be passed up to General Secretary Brezhnev and later Andropov. He pursued the same line as Andropov in denouncing American departure from détente and pursuit of military superiority and in reaffirming Soviet fidelity to a policy of détente, arms limitation, and peaceful coexistence. The only difference, but an important one, was that Chernenko did not share Andropov's assessment in 1983 that there was no possibility that the main adversary might return to a realistic evaluation of the correlation of forces and resume negotiation and détente with the Soviet Union.

It is not surprising that in 1984 the Soviet leaders would still be cautious and suspicious of American motivations in seeming to be prepared, after three years of harsh rhetoric and militant policies, to return to dialogue with its main adversary. When Ronald Reagan, beginning with his January 1984 speech, began to seek a serious dialogue (and later actual negotiations) with the Soviet leader—which, in fact, unknown even to most of his own administration except Secretary Shultz, he had begun in early 1983—not only Soviet leaders but also most Americans doubted Reagan's interest. (Neither political supporters of Reagan nor his opponents believed he would do such a thing.) Later, of course, it became clear that Reagan was indeed serious and that the "Reagan II" of his second term would resume and then go beyond his predecessors in developing relations with the Soviet Union. But in 1984 there was still a dominant assumption that the Reagan of the Committee on the Present Danger and of blatant hostility in his first three years in office would not end up in Moscow in 1988 dismissing his recent characterization of the Soviet Union as an evil empire as referring to a "different time."[38]

Throughout 1984 the Soviet leaders continued to see inconsistent signs of whether it would be possible to see a changing American relationship or whether, as Andropov had concluded, such hopes could only be "illusions." The VRYaN intelligence alert continued, with additional attention to real, suspected, or simply feared American efforts to promote active subversion of communist rule in the Soviet Union and Eastern Europe.[39]

There were no more incidents like the KAL 007 downing or potentially dangerous misinterpretations like the fears stirred by Able Archer. Even as he was seeking a serious dialogue, however, Reagan was unable to leave well enough alone. Before a radio broadcast on August 11, Reagan jokingly remarked into an open microphone: "My fellow Americans, I am pleased to tell you I have signed legislation to outlaw Russia forever. We begin bombing in five minutes." His levity over a matter of such gravity evoked widespread criticism, especially in Western Europe. It is not known whether any Soviet intelligence officer (whether overly intent or with a bold sense of humor) reported the event under VRYaN, but the Soviet leadership after three days of deliberation issued a statement objecting strongly to such "invective, unprecedentedly hostile to the USSR and dangerous to the cause of peace," adding that "such behavior is incompatible with the high responsibility borne by leaders of states, particularly nuclear powers, for the destinies of their own peoples and of all mankind." They also used the occasion to criticize American military doctrine and "military-political plans for securing US world domination" and calls for a "crusade." The incident soon faded away, although it added to the doubts in many minds (probably including those of at least some Soviet leaders) as to Reagan's sincerity in his election-year calls for a "dialogue" and protestations of wishing to improve relations with the Soviet Union.[40]

President Reagan was reelected, and it remained to be seen whether he really would make an effort to negotiate with Soviet leaders. Of course, no less important was whether the Soviet leadership would emerge from its geriatric shuffling and be prepared for its part to join in serious dialogue and diplomacy.

CHAPTER FIVE

Gorbachev
Back to Détente—and Beyond, 1985–91

In March 1985 Chernenko died. The Politburo decided on Mikhail Gorbachev, a vigorous young leader who during a visit to London in November 1984 had been praised by Prime Minister Margaret Thatcher as "a man we can do business with," as his successor. Reagan decided not to attend Chernenko's funeral, but he sent Vice President Bush (his third attendance at a Soviet leader's funeral in less than three years) and Secretary Shultz—and, with them, an invitation to Gorbachev for a summit meeting. In their brief encounter, Gorbachev told Bush, "We are not inherently enemies," but Bush did not respond. Before such a meeting was agreed upon, however, there were several months of cautious exchanges over the terms, especially concerning arms control (which in January Shultz and Gromyko had agreed in principle should be resumed). Although the Soviets had been seeking renewal of engagement and détente, it was not an easy decision in Moscow because there was no assurance that the United States was prepared to reach agreement on arms limitations or any other concrete steps to improve relations. But Gorbachev and Reagan both wished to meet, and after some rocky diplomatic exchanges and hesitation in Moscow, they agreed to a summit in Geneva. It was clear that Gorbachev had seized the reins of Soviet policy. One day before the world learned of the Geneva meeting, it was announced that Eduard Shevardnadze, another young Soviet leader who was

74

Gorbachev's friend and political ally, would become foreign minister (Gromyko became the USSR's titular president, chairman of the Presidium of the Supreme Soviet of the USSR). When Gorbachev and Reagan met in Geneva in November 1985, no major agreements were reached (indeed, the major issue of arms control and SDI was confirmed to be in deadlock). But the two men initiated a dialogue and recognized each other as real persons, not as cardboard images of ideological adversaries in the thrall of Wall Street or an evil empire.[1]

The most important effect of the Geneva summit, evident only in retrospect, was the launching of policy reevaluations, first in Moscow, then in Washington.[2] This process of reappraisal continued at the two leaders' second meeting, in Reykjavik, Iceland (chosen as midway between Moscow and Washington), in August 1986. Again, no agreements were reached, but unexpectedly radical possibilities for arms reductions were discussed. Both leaders began to see mutual interest in reconsidering not only far-reaching arms reductions but also the role of military power in the bilateral relationship. In fact, the change went even further: They were developing common aspirations for a radically changed US-Soviet political relationship.

Gorbachev's closest foreign affairs adviser, Anatoly Chernyayev, wrote in his diary that Reykjavik was the turning point in Gorbachev's evaluation of Reagan and of the opportunity for overcoming the Cold War. He no longer thought the USSR faced an imperialist military threat, and he never again spoke or thought of Wall Street capitalists running American policy behind a façade of politicians.[3] As had occurred with his predecessors, personal contact and communication with a literally personified "adversary" brought about changed perceptions and new policies.

Gorbachev's first encounters with Reagan, along with other contacts and reevaluation of Soviet relations with the West, convinced Gorbachev that radical changes were needed in order to end the arms race, US-Soviet hostility, and the Cold War.

Early in 1986, before he had been in power a year, Gorbachev laid out at the Twenty-Seventh Communist Party Congress a new conceptual basis for thinking about world affairs, becoming the first Soviet leader to proclaim that with problems "on a global scale affecting the very foundation of the existence of civilization . . . cooperation on a global scale is required." He spoke of "the interdependent and in many ways integral world that is taking shape"—*one* world.[4] In fact, after the congress, he stopped referring even to two different and opposed political systems. He also alluded to a novel conception of Soviet security that eschewed confrontation and military power. "The task of ensuring security increasingly is a political task," he told the congress, "and can be resolved only by political means." This statement prefigured radical policy steps unimagined by almost anyone in 1986. The Stalinist two-camp, two-world conception was now passé, and the foundation for seemingly endless arms programs had been removed.

"New thinking" (the literal translation of the term used by the Russians, *novoye myshleniye*) had arrived with breathtaking speed. And it led Gorbachev to another startling conclusion: The new world he wanted to bring into being could come about only if the Soviet Union took the lead and assumed the main burden of establishing different relations, an approach that he made a fundamental task of his foreign policy. He recognized that it was going to take not only dramatic proposals for arms reductions but also unilateral Soviet actions to stimulate Reagan into action on military détente. Gorbachev would meet three more times with Reagan and then four additional times with Bush, and surprising developments came one after another. Agreements, including a formal treaty destroying all intermediate-range nuclear ballistic missiles, and unilateral actions, such as greatly reducing the size of the Soviet Army and withdrawing a large portion of Soviet forces from Eastern Europe, peppered political leaders in both Western and communist regimes with novel challenges, forcing them to deal with major changes taken at Gorbachev's initiative.

Gorbachev's new thinking about Soviet foreign policy was grounded in decades of gradual change in Soviet evaluations of the world around the USSR and in Soviet policies to deal with that world, above all with the main adversary. Its roots were in Khrushchev's post-Stalin "thaw," including steps such as emphasizing peaceful coexistence. It also had been influenced by Western socialist and Eurocommunist ideas and by experiences gained from increased contacts with Western thinking and with life in the West, especially during the period of détente, which lasted into the 1980s in Europe.

Although some dissidents were involved in this conceptual transition, it was mainly accomplished by officials who came to view the world more pragmatically, including some of the best academics, journalists, and other professionals in the Academy of Social Sciences, the Central Committee's departments, and the Foreign Ministry.[5] There arose among them—especially among those who worked in institutions dealing directly with the outside world—a gradually growing recognition that they, and their country, were in a sense imprisoned by their ideology. They increasingly wanted the USSR to become part of the international community and not automatically see others as inherent adversaries. Moreover, many gradually realized that the Soviet Union had contributed to the Cold War and its tensions. Their subversion of Stalin-era views was slow to surface because official fealty to orthodoxy remained dominant into the 1980s, but the ideology had become increasingly brittle and pro forma. What brought change to the fore was the arrival in power of a Soviet leader willing to embrace the new thinking openly and use it as a basis for state policy. Gorbachev's deathblow to old thinking caused revolutionary change in international relations and tolled the final bell for the communist regimes in Eastern Europe—and the USSR.

Perhaps most surprising was the relatively large number of senior Communist Party functionaries in the Central Committee departments concerned with international affairs who readily took up new thinking. To be sure, some at the top (including candidate Politburo member Boris Ponomarev, for almost two decades head of the International Department), and some primarily concerned with Eastern

European communist parties, were strongly opposed, but they were retired. Several deputy chiefs of the International Department, however, including Vadim Zagladin, became valuable members of Gorbachev's team. So too did most of the senior consultants to the Central Committee departments, including former consultants now heading key institutes of the Academy of Sciences (Georgy Arbatov, Nikolai Inozemtsev, Yevgeny Primakov, and Oleg Bogomolov). Gorbachev's personal aide on foreign affairs, Anatoly Chernyayev, was a liberal new thinker notwithstanding many years' service in the International Department. Party leaders in the provinces, to be sure, were little engaged, but most simply followed the lead of the general secretary, Gorbachev, and bravely voiced new-thinking formulations while continuing to act on the basis of traditional old thinking.

As security was redefined to rely less on military power, the idea of giving up familiar military assets (and later geopolitical ones) in exchange for better relations with former adversaries was disturbing to many. Nonetheless, the military leadership was more prepared than many political party chiefs to adopt new military doctrine—including mutual deterrence—and engage in serious negotiations even with heavy Soviet concessions.[6]

The situation with respect to military institutions, military policy, and the role of the military under the new thinking differed importantly from the situation with respect to the intelligence establishment and the role of intelligence. To be sure, the United States and NATO were "the probable enemy" of the Soviet Union and Warsaw Pact in case of war, and the overwhelming preoccupation in peacetime military strategic planning is preparation for possible war. This was true for ideological, political, and above all existential geopolitical reasons—the United States was, after all, *the* other superpower and the only opponent who could challenge the Soviet Union in a nuclear duel. But there was a difference between being the "main adversary" in an ongoing intelligence war and a putative enemy in a possible war that by now no sensible planner on either side could regard as anything but a catastrophe for both sides if it were to occur.

The Soviet military leadership had long been seen as a notoriously conservative element, and yet in the mid- to late 1980s it demonstrated an unexpected ability to recognize and accept a fundamental change not only in military doctrine but also in strategy and in its force levels and deployment. While the "probable enemy" remained the same, the possibility of war was seen as realistically much lower than it had appeared even in the very recent past, with VRYaN in the early to mid-1980s hyping a dangerously looming surprise nuclear-missile attack. Moreover, the new Soviet foreign policy was working to lower still further politico-military tensions and the theoretical possibility of such an attack and to reduce the deployment and size of the counterposed military forces of the two alliances in Europe and in the strategic arms arsenals of the United States and the Soviet Union. Thus as Marshal Sergei Akhromeyev later put it, "the new [Soviet] foreign policy in the years 1986–1989 led simultaneously to a significant improvement in relations with the United States and the countries of Western Europe, to a lowering of military tensions, to a lessening of the military danger for the Soviet Union, and that was achieved not by military but by political means." He does observe that this was a "new and unusual" situation for the military leaders, for many "difficult" to comprehend and not understood by all. After all, the Soviet Union lost its allies and alliance as well as its forward deployment in Central and Eastern Europe that provided defense in depth, and it met with great practical difficulties of adjustment for redeployment and new training of the armed forces. "For us military men, 1986–1989 was a time of great shocks." Still, he considered the changes necessary.[7]

The change in military doctrine and strategy was made in 1986, formally ratified by the USSR Defense Council in December 1986, and announced after consultation with the Eastern European allies at a Warsaw Pact meeting in May 1987. By then it was already being implemented in the Soviet Union, for example, in new defensive military training exercises. The key change in military doctrine and strategy was drastic: Until 1986 Soviet strategy was to meet an enemy attack (and there were no variants calling for Soviet decision on initiation of a war) by active defense and, as soon as possible, transition to a massive counteroffensive striking deep into the West "to destroy the aggressor." From 1986 on, the new doctrine abandoned the concept of a prompt counteroffensive; in Akhromeyev's words, "we would repel aggression only by defensive operations and simultaneously seek with the assistance of political measures to liquidate the conflict."[8]

Underlying this momentous change in strategy was an even more fundamental change in the overall politico-military relationship. Until the change in 1986, military doctrine "took over" if war occurred: "The prevention of war was the fundamental task of Soviet *foreign* policy." Now "it had become ever more evident that by its nature the existing military doctrine was obsolete and required revision. Questions of the prevention of war must become the subject not only of *foreign* policy but also of *military* doctrine."[9] For example, the radical downsizing of the Soviet armed forces, their retraction from Central Europe, and other measures—partly by international agreement but also by unilateral action—could contribute to preventing war.

Needless to say, this radical revision of military doctrine and strategy was a shock to most Soviet military men—Akhromeyev has described the uproar it received when he first presented it to the General Staff Academy, with "stormy discussions" continuing there for more than a month. But Akhromeyev and the General Staff were, he says, "even proud" of their successful change to make the prevention of war a component of military doctrine.[10] Thus while the United States and NATO remained the "probable enemy" in a war, war itself was recognized to have become very improbable. With the prevention of war a military as well as political task, and with recognition that the United States too did not want a war, there was no probable enemy requiring a massive military counterweight for either deterrence or war-fighting, much less an active main adversary when the aim was tacit partnership in assuring that a war would never occur.

It should be noted that the principal exception to the remarkable transition in thinking in the Soviet military establishment was in the GRU, the Main Intelligence Directorate of the General Staff. The GRU did not of course have an independent position or express dissent; indeed it was sufficiently unimportant that it was not brought into the deliberations of the General Staff leaders. Nonetheless, former GRU officers have reported that even after the new doctrine was adopted and massive changes were undertaken in the military forces, GRU leaders and especially its communications intelligence service continued to treat more seriously than their KGB colleagues (and rivals) the otherwise almost forgotten VRYaN exercise right down to 1991 (and its underlying suspicions even after).

New thinking included prominently a disavowal of the very concept of an adversarial relationship, seeing in a political confrontation bolstered by nuclear deterrence a real danger of war. The "image of the enemy" was now seen as itself contributing to enmity and therefore as something to be discarded—on both sides. This was a drastic change, but the old image was not compatible with the conception of one world and the need for cooperation in dealing with global problems—energy, ecology, the economy, and not least security. Security was now defined as eliminating threats of war and reliance on nuclear weapons, and as "common security" for all. In practice the Soviet Union and the United States had been uneasy partners as well as adversaries during much of the Cold War, but now partnership was to be integral to the relationship even though competition and sometimes opposing interests remained. A fundamentally adversarial relationship was simply not compatible with the new outlook.

As Gorbachev's foreign policy aide has noted, from the very outset in early 1986 the new thinking embraced a whole panoply of related guidelines for policy—"recognition of the impermissibility of nuclear confrontation and war, breaking the arms race and beginning disarmament, a new look at the very logic of Soviet foreign policy based on international class struggle, rejection of the 'image of the enemy,' and recognition of the absence of an imperialist threat to the USSR."[11] As another of the new thinkers put it to me in 1985, they now realized that the danger of war came not from imperialism but from the very existence of adversarial confrontation and deterrence based on alert nuclear weapons. The main adversaries of the Cold War needed to become main partners—which of course required realization and action by both sides.

In a meeting in Moscow in October 1987 looking toward another summit meeting, Gorbachev challenged Secretary of State George Shultz: "Can't you [Americans] get along without continuing to portray the Soviet Union as an enemy? How can we continue to negotiate with you if you see us as an enemy?"[12]

At a major leadership conference sponsored by the Foreign Ministry in July 1988, Shevardnadze and two of his chief deputies spoke about the need to eliminate "the image of the enemy."[13] One of them, First Deputy Minister Anatoly Kovalev, emphasized that apart from encouraging and making it easier for the West to abandon such a perception of Soviet policy, "we ourselves have so far done little to demolish the analogous stereotype in the consciousness of the Soviet people. One without the other will hardly succeed."[14] In a mischievous twist, Georgy Arbatov on several occasions in the late 1980s, including one I personally recall, expressed this serious idea to Americans in a jocular way: "We are going to do something terrible to you—we are going to take away your Enemy!"

Intelligence played no role in promoting the new thinking that fundamentally recast Soviet policy. Soviet foreign intelligence had to adapt to new assignments in objectives, collection, reporting, and evaluations—above all with respect to the main adversary. As Communist Party leader, Gorbachev of course received a steady flow of intelligence selected by the KGB, the GRU, and Central Committee departments. Kryuchkov, head of the KGB's foreign intelligence when Gorbachev took power, records in his memoir that Gorbachev from the outset "showed great interest in [intelligence] information" and that he "was, one could say, greedy for it."[15] Partly for this reason but mainly because the political leadership had become so ossified, the intelligence chiefs welcomed Gorbachev's accession to power.[16] At the same time, they noted later that he often failed to apply intelligence in policymaking—at least not as the KGB chiefs believed it should be applied.[17]

Kryuchkov and KGB intelligence analysts did try to be responsive to the changes in policy under the new thinking. A former KGB intelligence officer with service in the United States has suggested that Kryuchkov sought to find a way to depict the United States as not too aggressive but at the same time as dangerous from the standpoint of Soviet interests.[18] Speaking at the Foreign Ministry conference in 1988 shortly before his promotion to chairmanship of the KGB, Kryuchkov tried to accommodate what he called the Communist Party's "new methodology for looking at the world" and even acknowledged the impact of new Soviet policies in the West: "The 'enemy image,' the image of the Soviet state as a 'totalitarian,' 'half-civilized' society, is being eroded and our ideological and political opponents are recognizing the profound nature of our reforms and their beneficial effect on foreign policy." But he balanced that observation with doubt about the depth of the US commitment to disarmament and with concern about the ongoing US-Soviet intelligence war, alleging there had been "in the first half of this year more than 900 provocation operations" (i.e., attempts to recruit agents) and "agent penetration into key Soviet installations such as the Ministry of Defense, the KGB, and the Ministry of Foreign Affairs." He even cited a familiar, but by 1988 rarely mentioned, danger—"the immediate danger of nuclear conflict being unleashed"—which he ambiguously described as a "*former*" KGB tasking requirement but one that has "not been removed from the agenda."[19] This was a last-gasp reference to the VRYaN alert system.[20]

Overall, as chairman of the KGB from October 1988 to August 1991, Kryuchkov displayed a notably less strident record in his public statements than had his predecessors, Andropov and Viktor Chebrikov. He did not again refer to the possibility of an enemy nuclear attack or to Western intelligence provocations. He continued to offer rhetorical support to new thinking.[21] But he did not basically change the role or policies of the KGB.

The KGB could not basically reform. It had existed (under various names) for almost seventy years to engage enemies in mortal combat, and if the enemies were now declared not to exist, it lost its own raison d'être. Of course, it continued to ferret out Western political, military, and scientific/technical secrets and to provide support to the leadership in its foreign policy (albeit still in its accustomed way). And new tasks included seeking to identify Western opposition to renewed détente and to new thinking in the West as well as to Soviet initiatives. Its dire warnings of external threats were no longer needed, however, and its "active measures" against the United States had to give way to some support of constructive relations.

The KGB thus tried, largely unsuccessfully, to take up Gorbachev's new thinking in foreign policy, seeking to persuade the leadership that it had been converted to it. Its annual report to Gorbachev for the year 1988 declared that it was "actively supporting the foreign policy of the Soviet state and has *adjusted its activity* with the aim of making a greater contribution to resolving the tasks of creating a universal system of international security and favorable conditions for deepening the processes of *perestroika* in the country."[22] From the available evidence, however, although KGB analysts sometimes addressed matters of interest to Gorbachev, they often cast doubt on Western readiness to cooperate and thus undercut the protestations of support for Soviet policies. Vadim Bakatin, the last head of the KGB (from August into December 1991), concluded after reviewing its reports that "the information that the KGB provided to the Soviet political leadership did not help to curb the arms race, or to enhance trust between states"—key objectives of Gorbachev's policy.[23]

Throughout 1985–86 there continued to be many incidents involving the "intelligence war" between the two sides, but they did not have the effect on the changing basic relationship that they previously would have had. Gorbachev, in particular, was not led to change his course of new thinking and political reformation.[24]

Gorbachev's early interest in intelligence reports quickly declined. On November 29, 1985, Gorbachev had his Politburo colleagues discuss a memorandum "on the impermissibility of distortions of the actual state of affairs in communications and informational reports submitted to the Central Committee and other ruling bodies." The Communist Party organization itself was under fire. One result was to instruct the KGB to take measures to ensure that its information was accurate. The record of a follow-up meeting of the KGB leadership shows that all KGB components were tasked with taking "all necessary measures to preclude sending to [the leadership of] the KGB of the USSR unreliable information and non-objective evaluations of the state of affairs in concrete sectors and lines of operational service."[25] Gorbachev was not satisfied with the results.

In May 1987 Gorbachev convened KGB, GRU, and Foreign Ministry intelligence analytical chiefs and sharply criticized their performance. A former KGB officer reports the meeting had little impact; the head of the PGU's Information-Analytical Department simply told his people to improve their analysis.[26] Chernyayev cites from his diary a comment Gorbachev made in the spring of 1989 to a small circle of advisers (including General Kryuchkov) about the intelligence the leadership was receiving: "Reading a cabled report I immediately recognize the 'fingerprint'—whether it is GRU, the KGB, the MID [Foreign Ministry] or the Party staff. Each has 'its own interests.' But we, the leadership, need to know the truth in order to make correct decisions. . . . I'm looking at you, Vladimir Aleksandrovich [addressing Kryuchkov]!"[27]

The value of intelligence reporting and analysis to the political leadership was also diminished by the KGB practice, in the name of security, of providing only vague indications of information sources, often referring simply to a "reliable source" or "documentary evidence." The source might indeed be a trusted agent or an acquired document, but the information might also have come from a newspaper article, gossip, or a source's (or his case officer's) assumptions or beliefs. It might even have been invented out of whole cloth by the case officer, the *rezident*, the Center's information analysts, or Kryuchkov himself.

Gen. Nikolai Leonov, the head of the Information-Analytical Department of the PGU from 1973 to 1984, described its task as "filtering the flow of information in accordance with its significance and quality, systematically collecting the data and analyzing the collected documentation"—not intelligence assessment or estimates as understood in the United States.[28]

Although Gorbachev discounted much KGB reporting as distorted by self-interest or ideological correctness or as policy lobbying, he was sometimes susceptible to reporting that alleged continued Western "old thinking" skeptical about his policies. In January 1989, dismayed that Bush had not responded to his dramatic UN speech the previous month, he told Italian Communist Party leader Achille Ochetto that Bush "has in mind a Western effort to undermine the Soviet Union's international initiatives." And in April he was receptive to a Kryuchkov report that the CIA and State Department had created a commission aimed at discrediting Gorbachev and his policies; he even raised the matter in conversations with UK prime minister Margaret Thatcher and Italian prime minister Giulio Andreotti, both of whom tried to reassure him.[29] Only at his meeting with Bush in Malta in December 1989 were Gorbachev's suspicions dispelled. (Even then, Bush himself said at Malta that he had "turned 180 degrees from my previous position" and now fully supported Gorbachev, so the Soviet leader may have considered his earlier doubts valid.) Gorbachev probably also considered his policies to have been successful in altering the president's thinking even if he thought Bush had not completely abandoned his image of Gorbachev as an adversary, as is suggested in the Soviet leader's comment that "the United States and the USSR are 'doomed' [destined] to talk, cooperate and collaborate. There is no other way. But for that we have to rid ourselves of seeing each other as enemies."[30]

Just as intelligence had not been active in the development of new thinking, so it remained on the sidelines as new thinking manifested itself in new policies. Gorbachev selected Kryuchkov to head the KGB in 1988, promoted him to the rank of general of the army, and in 1989 brought him into the Politburo. He met with him fairly frequently but did not bring him into policy discussions, nor did he rely upon intelligence beyond routine acceptance of reporting. General Leonov, one of the more astute intelligence chiefs, observed, beginning in 1986, a noticeable loss of interest by Gorbachev in intelligence, including even espionage successes: "Intelligence lost its consumers, and the consumers lost interest in intelligence." Gorbachev increasingly ignored intelligence when it was different from what he wanted to believe. As General Shebarshin put it, "when the information confirmed Gorbachev's views, it was welcome. But when policy and reality started to diverge, with the situation in the country going from bad to worse, Gorbachev did not want to know."[31] By 1991, Leonov sadly noted, "foreign intelligence was no longer in the focus of the Government's [i.e., Gorbachev's] attention."[32]

The Soviet intelligence chiefs were of course keenly aware of their growing lack of influence and, indeed, relevance. General Leonov, one of the more astute (if also ultimately conservative) among them, has noted that beginning in 1986 he observed a sharp loss of interest by Gorbachev and the leadership in intelligence. He noted a decline in political "tasking" (assignments to obtain intelligence on specific subjects), a lack of feedback, and a breakdown in mutual understanding among institutions—for example, between KGB intelligence and the foreign ministry, intelligence and the defense establishment—and relationships with the divided Central Committee staffs. Leonov also mentions (without explaining) a sharp falling-off in information received from KGB posts and embassies abroad.[33]

In July 1990, at the Twenty-Eighth (and final) Communist Party Congress, the party relationship with the Soviet government was severed. One consequence was that KGB intelligence was no longer sent even to the Politburo or International Department of the Central Committee. Even earlier, the annual report of the KGB to Gorbachev covering 1989 (dated February 14, 1990) was addressed to him as chairman of the Supreme Soviet of the USSR rather than as general secretary of the Central Committee of the Communist Party of the Soviet Union.[34]

Beginning in mid-June 1991, by order of General Kryuchkov, the same KGB reports sent to Gorbachev (with a few exceptions) were also sent to the new president of the Russian Republic, Boris Yeltsin. General Shebarshin, chief of foreign intelligence, has acknowledged that he helped persuade Kryuchkov that Gorbachev would never win against Yeltsin and that Yeltsin was the best bet for preserving the union—their principal concern. Kryuchkov, who still had some hopes for Gorbachev, reluctantly agreed and ordered that intelligence be regularly provided to Yeltsin and that contacts be maintained with Yeltsin and his colleagues in the Russian Republic leadership.[35]

Gorbachev hardly ever refers in his memoir and other publications to intelligence inputs to policymaking. In talking with George Shultz in 1987, he did comment favorably on the overall role of intelligence in allowing each side to know the other better: "We are political leaders, not babes. We know why the CIA was created and what it does. You gather intelligence on us, and we gather intelligence on you. I'll say even more: the fact that you know a lot about us introduces an element of stability. It's better to know a lot about one another than only a little. . . . Intelligence, in its usual meaning [i.e., secret information], plays a constructive role by helping to avert precipitous political or military actions." He also indicated, however, that in playing this positive role, the Soviet and American ambassadors were "our intelligence chiefs, thank God!"[36] He clearly did not regard KGB reporting as a major source of key political information or assessment.

Gorbachev and some other Soviet leaders learned to discount or ignore intelligence reports, sometimes because they did not support their policy preferences, other times because they suspected they were of questionable validity or deliberately slanted or fabricated. In August 1990, when Iraq had occupied Kuwait and the United States was seeking international support to press Iraq to withdraw, the KGB, in an attempt to head off a joint US-Soviet stand, gave Gorbachev a false report that the United States was about to strike Iraq. Gorbachev and Shevardnadze ignored this report, which Gorbachev saw as a deliberate attempt to stymie Soviet policy—as indeed it was.[37] General Grushko, first deputy chief of the KGB, discusses another case of manipulation in his memoir in the course of complaining that Gorbachev ignored valid intelligence to which he should have paid attention. Gorbachev was seeking Western economic aid at a G-7 meeting in June 1991 amid public speculation about sizable Western credits to the USSR, and the KGB had concrete, accurate intelligence that the Western powers *had* decided *not* to provide such assistance. Gorbachev, burned before by bad information and believing the KGB was out to derail his policy with fabricated reporting, did not accept this intelligence as valid. In this case, the KGB had gilded the lily of good data by adding a false claim, telling Gorbachev it was part of a Western *disinformation* campaign to make him think he would get aid, which was not the case.[38]

Another problem KGB officers faced was that they often were not players in supporting important negotiations. General Leonov, longtime head of the Information-Analytical Department of the KGB's foreign intelligence service, records that the KGB was not tasked to help prepare for the 1986 Reykjavik summit. The KGB nonetheless volunteered materials, Leonov states, including a correct assessment that Reagan was not prepared to give in on SDI, leading Leonov to complain, "Obviously, our materials were not taken into account."[39] In this case, Gorbachev was already well aware SDI was a likely US sticking point, but he wanted to open up the subject, and for that purpose the Defense Ministry and the Foreign Ministry materials were more relevant. Another example showing KGB irrelevance to issues important to Gorbachev was the role of the Defense Ministry in facilitating Gorbachev's offer in January 1986 of a comprehensive program for eliminating all nuclear weapons by the year 2000. In this case the proposal was based on a study by the General Staff;

some key military leaders were more prepared than other officials to engage in negotiations aimed at surrendering military assets in exchange for anticipated lowered threats from adversaries.[40] Gorbachev intended his proposal to be a serious opening to a basic improvement in relations through building confidence based on progressively greater arms limitations and reductions, even if the goal of complete elimination of nuclear weapons was too much to agree upon in the foreseeable future.[41]

The May 1987 meeting at which Gorbachev criticized the analytical work of all the intelligence agencies may well have prompted discussion of whether the very conception of a main adversary was still valid. Several senior KGB officials have said that the question arose at about that time. At the same July 1988 conference at which Shevardnadze talked about giving up the image of the enemy, while KGB chief Kryuchkov spoke of the need to erode the *Western* "image of the enemy" applied to the USSR, he made no reference to a need to dispense with the *Soviet* "image of the enemy" applied to the West and above all to the United States.[42] But change was coming. Looking back, senior KGB officers have acknowledged they gave in to the change, albeit reluctantly. Writing long after the Cold War, General Kirpichenko noted: "Former friends and former adversaries have become partners. Ceasing to be someone's enemies, we rather calmly have rejected the concept of a 'main adversary.' The epoch of confrontation and hostility, it has turned out, could be ended."[43] General Shebarshin, however, noted in his memoir that it had been difficult to give up the concept and that dropping the designation of the main adversary for the United States came only after a long and serious debate, with considerable opposition in the KGB. He nonetheless stated that with the Paris CSCE summit meeting the Cold War was over, and there was no longer doubt that the concept of a main adversary was also over.[44] At that meeting, on November 26, 1990, the United States and its NATO allies, together with the Soviet Union and its Warsaw Pact allies, formally signed a statement agreeing that they were "no longer adversaries." Gorbachev's statement to Bush in December 1989 at Malta that "we don't consider you an enemy any more" had finally elicited the Western reaction he had sought."[45]

With the fading of the image of the enemy and of the concept of the main adversary, the external threat to the Soviet Union was seen as greatly diminished. This facilitated Gorbachev's policies of unilateral and negotiated reductions of military forces and redefinition of military requirements, including acceptance of momentous changes in Central and Eastern Europe. A month after the Paris summit, a Soviet journalist noted an important double-edged implication of the change: "We have lost our beloved enemy, whose existence guaranteed the economic and political interests of vast segments of Soviet society."[46] It was unsurprising that resistance to the new situation came not only from intelligence professionals but also from the military-industrial complex. On one occasion, Gorbachev reproached Oleg Baklanov, the head of the Defense Industry Department of the Central Committee (and later one of the abortive putsch leaders), telling him sternly, "You only see the United States through a gunsight." Baklanov unhesitatingly shot back, "Yes!"[47]

For the KGB, which was responsible for internal security in the face of growing unrest and other public expressions of dissatisfaction that eventually led to the USSR's collapse, it is hardly surprising that senior officers looked for and "found" foreign—including American—support for internal political dissidence, nationality conflicts, separatism, and other threatening activities. KGB chiefs repeatedly warned about the dangers of subversion and unrest, and many have also since alleged (and cited what they see as evidence of) Western intelligence support for this internal threat.[48] General Kryuchkov, for example, writes that in 1989 the KGB "received reliable information on the activities of the special [i.e., intelligence] services of Western countries against the Soviet Union and all of its union republics," which had "sharply heightened collection of information on the situation in our country." He further contends that as trouble in the country grew in 1990 and 1991, Western services stepped up incitement of nationality issues and engaged in "economic sabotage."[49] But nowhere does he define what kind of "reliable information" was allegedly obtained. From reading many KGB reports, some sent to Gorbachev, it seemed clear to me that ambiguity about the validity of these charges characterized the original reporting as well as Kryuchkov's memoir. It is not surprising that Gorbachev ignored such reports.

According to General Grushko, the KGB told Gorbachev that the United States had concluded that Soviet concessions to extremist and national separatist demands would lead to chaos in the USSR. He cites this as an example of the "dire warnings" the KGB had provided to the leadership. Gorbachev, who had already calculated the risks of making—or failing to make—concessions, probably dismissed such warnings as lobbying. Grushko also claimed that the KGB had "reliable data on the fact that the US and NATO greatly counted on weakening the Soviet Union" and that "in the Soviet Union the Americans supported any striving for separatism under cover of the slogan of democratization."[50] He did not, however, provide any such data.

The most vituperative KGB attack alleging American attempts to break up the Soviet Union was made in April 1991 by the KGB's analysis chief, General Leonov, in addressing (at Kryuchkov's suggestion) a caucus of ultraconservative parliamentarians (the Soyuz, or Union, faction). Leonov ranted about US attempts to destroy the USSR and virtually charged Gorbachev with ignoring intelligence warnings and imperiling the country as Stalin had in 1941: "The KGB has been informing the leadership of the country about this in a timely and detailed way. We would not want a repetition of the tragic situation before the Great Fatherland War against Germany [World War II], when Soviet intelligence warned about the imminent attack of Nazi Germany, but Stalin rejected this information as wrong and even provocative. You know what that mistake cost us. . . . *History will not forgive us for passivity and inaction.*"[51]

This remarkable statement by Leonov, who had only recently

been placed in charge of analysis and information for the entire KGB, was a sign of the hard-line faction's desperate desire to reverse Gorbachev's policies. Early in Gorbachev's tenure, many Soviet intelligence leaders had accepted his ambitious goals of managing the economy better, disengaging from costly foreign entanglements, and even enlarging personal liberties. But they became increasingly concerned by 1988 and 1989 that these goals had been pursued with insufficient attention to maintaining Soviet security. By 1990–91 most intelligence chiefs were alarmed over the deteriorating internal situation and what they saw as foreign policy failures (especially German reunification in NATO and the disintegration of the Soviet politico-military position in Europe).

The paranoia of the KGB's chiefs contributed to the USSR's final crisis. In June 1991 there was an unsuccessful attempt in the USSR's parliament, the Supreme Soviet, by several of Gorbachev's closest colleagues at a "soft coup," which would have taken many of Gorbachev's powers away from him.[52] In the course of it, Kryuchkov cited a 1977 KGB report that contended the United States was embarking on a program to infiltrate and recruit Soviet citizens who could be trained and aided to become influential Soviet officials and eventually manipulate Soviet policies to serve American interests. By dragging this report out of the files, Kryuchkov hoped to suggest that CIA agents of influence were influencing Gorbachev's policies.[53]

Subversion and incitement were not the only charges made by the Soviet intelligence establishment against the main adversary in 1990–91 (and later in memoirs and histories). The six-volume history of Russian intelligence sponsored by the Russian Foreign Intelligence Service included in its final volume (issued in 2005) an unusual essay on the Reagan administration's program for defeating the Soviet Union. The essay described a three-part plan, said to have been launched in 1981–82, comprising a "triad" of objectives to defeat the Soviet Union and win the Cold War. The first objective was to reduce the sphere of influence of the USSR in the world, using "when necessary" direct military pressure, with three major targets:

Poland, Afghanistan, and the Cold War conflicts in the Third World. The second objective was described as shaking the foundations of the USSR internally through CIA actions. Third was a "merciless" economic trade war against the USSR with the objective of creating bankruptcy and an economic collapse through trade restrictions (especially in high technology and energy resources). The essay was unique in two respects. It was devoted, unlike all the other essays in the six volumes, not to Russian (including Soviet) intelligence experience but to an adversary's political and intelligence strategy against the Soviet Union. And, also unlike the other essays, it was based not on Russian/Soviet intelligence evaluations but on a single foreign source: the book *Victory* by Peter Schweizer. This author is an ardent supporter of Reagan's crusade against the "evil empire" and believer in Reagan's victory for the United States in the Cold War, not through his cooperation with Gorbachev but through a successful pursuit of something along the lines of the strategy described in Schweizer's book and in this Russian essay. The essay is not, however, reflective of the former Soviet intelligence chiefs' views.[54]

Although Soviet intelligence leaders have maintained in memoirs published since the Cold War that there were real American and other Western efforts to weaken the Soviet Union, they have also almost unanimously asserted that the main causes of the USSR's collapse were internal failings of the system and the leadership.[55] In 1990–91, without addressing their concerns openly, they sought to persuade Gorbachev and other leaders of the external threat. After the end of the Cold War, even while clinging to an instinctive distrust of America, they recognized openly what they were unwilling to say at the time. General Kirpichenko, for example, stated, "The bitter truth is that not the US Central Intelligence Agency, and not its 'agents of influence in the USSR,' but we ourselves destroyed our great state, and all our highest party and state figures continued to pursue chimeras, not wishing to distinguish myths from reality."[56]

The Main Adversary, it turned out, was not the main threat.

Conclusions

How did Soviet leaders move from seeing the world as two hostile camps with one destined to overcome the other to seeing it as a single entity sharing a common destiny? A key part of the explanation is the decline of the influence of ideology in the crucible of geopolitical realism and decades of interactions with the main adversary and other Western powers. Even the most ideologically influenced Soviet leaders of the Cold War, Stalin and Khrushchev, allowed pragmatism to guide policies despite the continuing influence of ideology in shaping their appraisals and the assessments prepared for them by their intelligence services. Ideology led to the decision to designate a main adversary, but it did not provide a formula for how to deal with it.

The most important factor leading Soviet and American leaders toward pragmatic realism was the advent of nuclear weapons. Both sides built such weapons in great numbers so as not to become vulnerable to hostile political leverage or outright attack, but they also had to prevent their use in order to ensure survival. Because of the possibility of escalation to the nuclear level, all wars directly involving the two main adversaries had to be avoided, and containing the tensions associated with sometimes intense political conflicts became a supreme imperative for leaders on both sides.

Critical to the drastic final changes in Soviet policy was the maturation of a generation of officials who grew up questioning Soviet reality in ways that led them to see the old ideology as not just an increasingly unconvincing outdated façade but also as an obstacle to necessary change. Ideology continued to serve a legitimizing function for the political system, and paradoxically it justified Gorbachev's authority, as general secretary of the Communist Party, to introduce radically new policies. In the end, however, its hold on Soviet views of foreign affairs faded as new thinking finally ground away some of its basic assumptions, including the need for a main adversary.

The end of the long US run as the USSR's main adversary in a cold war derived from the even more basic change of seeing the world as one, and one can see in retrospect that the path to that radical conception had been prepared by many years of Soviet diplomacy. Stalin had acknowledged the need for mixed rather than wholly adversarial relations with the main imperialist states, and the transition after his death marked a turning point of greater importance than either his successors or their Western adversaries appreciated at the time. Under Khrushchev, earlier orthodoxy was bent to take into account the impact of nuclear weapons and the inescapable reality that nuclear war could not serve any ideological or political purpose. Orthodox views of adversarial US-Soviet competition were cited in the 1970s but posed no obstacle to US-Soviet détente as Brezhnev and his colleagues sought international recognition of the USSR as a nuclear superpower capable of matching the influence of the United States. The shift of views as successive Soviet leaders moderated their images of American leaders was not uniform. Molotov, Andropov, and Kryuchkov demonized US leaders, sometimes using intelligence to support their views while in fact basing their evaluations on ideological prescription (Molotov) or fears (Andropov and Kryuchkov).

To be sure, many factors sustained the near half-century of cold war. Interests and objectives clashed, as did each side's perceptions and evaluations of its principal adversary. Persistent interactions and mutual misperceptions stimulated by ideological presumptions validated judgments about the adversary that perpetuated competition and confrontation. This study examined one side of the relationship, but the views it describes were part of a complex interrelationship of the actions, perceptions, and evaluations on *both* sides. Common to both sides was a perceived need for an adversary. As Georgy Arbatov put it, "the formation of an 'image of the enemy' was always important, even a key component of the policy of the 'Cold War.' It was possible to start it and then sustain it for decades as the centerpiece of the whole system of relations only under one condition—if the people believe in the existence of an aroused fear, and if possible also a detestable adversary."[1]

The ideological narrative influencing Soviet perceptions paradoxically also shaped US perceptions as American leaders recognized the importance of ideology in Soviet thinking and concluded it was necessary for the United States to counter the Soviet challenge. For both sides, intelligence was avidly sought and used to evaluate the adversary. At the same time, the prevailing image of an enemy profoundly affected the collection and interpretation of data by intelligence services and hence the assessments they offered political leaders. When year after year in the 1980s Soviet intelligence could find no real signs of Western preparation to attack, their chiefs, rather than congratulating their staffs for reassuring Moscow, urged them to redouble efforts to find evidence that was not there. The adversarial image trumped reality.

Even when an adversary's intentions are prejudged to be generally hostile and dangerous, they are nonetheless elusive—if not illusory. In such circumstances, intelligence does what it *can* do—derive an evaluation of intentions from capabilities. Nuclear deterrence, which served a defensive purpose, required a superoffensive capability since the requirement was to be able to retaliate in kind after absorbing an enemy attack. It is therefore unsurprising that intelligence services on both sides viewed and depicted such a capability by the *other* side as posing an offensive threat. On the Soviet side, when Western leaders spoke of pursuing a policy of deterrence, the term was consistently translated—for the Soviet leadership as well as publicly—as *ustrasheniye*, a word that connotes offensive intimidation or compellence. When Soviet leaders began to describe their own policy as deterrence, however, the word always used was *sderzhivaniye*, which connotes restraining a possible aggressor. The adversarial nature of the Cold War guaranteed that political leaders and intelligence officers on each side would tend to depict the other side in the worst possible light. Only after the advent of new thinking in the late 1980s did Soviet commentaries use the more defensive term to describe American deterrence policy.[2]

Until broken by Gorbachev, the assumption that the US-Soviet relationship *had* to be adversarial had pernicious influence not only in sustaining suspicion and massive investment in military power to deter an attack by the other side but also in distorting evaluations of the motives and policies of the putative enemy on a wide range of issues. It led to a tendency to see the adversary's motives and objectives as set and unchanging and thus to underestimate the impact of other parties or of one's own actions. It also tended, even when attempts were made to place oneself in the other side's shoes, to skew consideration of the other side's motives or options toward the more threatening or offensive end of the spectrum of possibilities.

One of the most explicit statements of recognition of the radically changed appreciation of the abandonment of the Cold War paradigm was made by Col. Gen. Nikolai Chervov of the General Staff in the authoritative journal *Military Thought* in mid-1990 in an article "On the Path to Trust and Security," with the superheading "New Thinking in Military Affairs." Chervov went so far as to acknowledge that the US and NATO Cold War doctrine of containment and deterrence "at one stage played a not unhelpful role in preserving peace. But new times require new policies." Chervov noted that containment and deterrence must be abandoned by both sides because that approach to seeking security "inherently embodies the conception of an evil enemy, the idea of confrontational mutual threat, mutual distrust, suspicion and hostility, a competition in mounting nuclear armaments."[3]

General Kirpichenko reported in 1993 that Russia's Foreign Intelligence Service had "renounced the very concept of 'an adversary.' Today, Russian intelligence does not have a main or even secondary adversaries."[4] Similarly, the Russian military doctrine adopted in 1993 specifically stated that "the Russian Federation does not regard any state as its enemy."[5]

Intelligence did not play the primary role in shaping basic Soviet perceptions of the United States. In the final analysis, the Soviet experience in evaluating its main adversary in the Cold War depended on judgments made by Soviet political leaders that were informed increasingly over time by their own experience, especially in direct contacts with American and other Western political leaders. Although until Gorbachev they had quite limited exposure to the outside world, such contacts as they had, especially with Western leaders, were all the more important to their understanding, on balance outweighing inputs by intelligence officers, diplomats, or Communist Party apparatchiks. Few Politburo members other than the top leaders had significant interactions with the outside world. The Soviet leader with the most experience involving intelligence, Andropov, had no significant contact with the West and none with Western leaders. Not surprisingly, he was the most consistently suspicious and fearful leader. Although professional Soviet foreign intelligence officers became more knowledgeable and effective in the 1970s and 1980s, senior intelligence chiefs in Moscow rarely had experience in the West. (By contrast, leading Foreign Ministry figures almost all had considerable such experience.) Where intelligence did play a role was in providing a great deal of specific and valuable information about the main adversary's military technology, military operational planning, diplomatic measures, and various aspects of political information, albeit often accompanied by weak analysis, especially in assessments and estimates of basic US policies and intentions. Intelligence did not contribute to understanding the adversary.

The most extensive and significant experience of any Soviet leader with the West and his Western counterparts was that of Gorbachev, who developed rapport with Reagan at Reykjavik and Bush at Malta. His experience contributed to the development of his new thinking on international matters, and he understood that changes in American thinking were needed to radically transform the US-Soviet relationship. He was not as naive as some of his Russian critics have suggested, although he was overly optimistic in counting on American acceptance of common values as a basis for relations. He expected, for example, that after the dismantling of the Warsaw Pact, the United States, rather than expanding NATO, would help build a common European security structure encompassing Soviet as well as Western interests. Where he broke decisively from his predecessors was in seeing positive potentialities in a drastically different East-West relationship and in acting on that prospect. The depth of his conviction that the United States and the West were not necessarily adversaries surprised many, as did his determination not only to argue his point of view but also to prove it in the real world. His willingness to take bold actions based on new thinking about international affairs brought about not only the end of the Main Adversary as a conceptual polar star of Soviet policy but also the end of the Cold War.

Resentment in Moscow in recent years over lost superpower status, the continuing global role of the United States, and perceived American disregard for Russian interests in expanding NATO contributes to raising tensions. But it does not represent a renewed Cold War. In the absence of an ideological commitment to a historically destined revolutionary change of the world order, there is no preordained struggle to the death between two political systems or two main adversaries. Russian leaders perceive the United States to be competitive and adversarial with respect to some Russian interests, but they do not see it as necessarily a permanent adversary, nor do they live in fear of a sudden American nuclear attack or, for that matter, of any war with the United States. Instead, the United States has come to occupy a prominent place as the most powerful of a number of important countries with which Russia is variously partner, competitor, or adversary—depending on issues and events. And Russian leaders pursue a traditional policy of seeking to protect and to advance its national interests, as they see them.

Today, a quarter century after the end of the Cold War, conflicts of interest and reciprocated suspicions have arisen. Vladimir Putin has seen not only a challenge to his desire to restore a weakened Russia to the status of a great power but also an opportunity to gain personal authority at home by belligerent challenges abroad and specifically by provoking a degree of hostility toward the United States. He has spurned American attempts to "reset" and reestablish a more favorable mutual relationship. But it is not a declaration of cold war nor a reconstitution of the danger of possible mutual extinction represented by the twentieth-century Cold War between two systems predestined to conflict and headed by two Main Adversaries.

Appendix 1

Soviet Leaders, 1945–91

Josef Stalin	1928–53
Georgy M. Malenkov	1953–57
Vyacheslav M. Molotov	
Nikolai A. Bulganin	
Nikita S. Khrushchev	
Nikita S. Khrushchev	1957–64
Leonid I. Brezhnev	1964–82
Yury V. Andropov	1982–84
Konstantin U. Chernenko	1984–85
Mikhail S. Gorbachev	1985–91

Appendix 2

Heads of the Soviet State Security Organization, 1945–91

Vsevolod N. Merkulov	NKGB/MGB	1943–46
Viktor S. Abakumov	MGB	1946–51
Semyon D. Ignatyev	MGB	1951–53
Lavrenty P. Beria	MVD	1953 (March–June)
Sergei N. Kruglov	MVD	1953–54
Ivan A. Serov	KGB	1954–58
Aleksandr N. Shelepin	KGB	1958–61
Vladimir Ye. Semichastny	KGB	1961–67
Yury V. Andropov	KGB	1967–82
Vitaly V. Fedorchuk	KGB	1982 (May–December)
Viktor M. Chebrikov	KGB	1982–88
Vladimir A. Kryuchkov	KGB	1988–91
Vadim V. Bakatin	KGB	1991 (August 23– December 19)

Key:

KGB	Committee for State Security
MGB	Ministry of State Security
MVD	Ministry of Internal Affairs
NKGB	People's Commissariat for State Security

Appendix 3

Heads of Soviet Foreign Intelligence, 1945–91

Pavel M. Fitin	INU (NKGB/MGB)	1939–46
Pyotr N. Kubatkin	PGU (MGB)	June–Sept. 1946
Pyotr V. Fedotov	PGU (MGB)	1946–47
	KI (deputy chairman)	1947–49
Sergei R. Savchenko	KI (deputy chairman)	1949–51
	PGU (MGB)	1951–52
Yevgeny P. Pitovranov	PGU (MGB)	1952–53
Vasily S. Ryasnoy	PGU (MVD)	March–June 1953
Aleksandr S. Panyushkin	PGU (MVD)	1953–54
	PGU (KGB)	1954–55
Aleksandr M. Sakharovsky	PGU (KGB)	1956–71
Fyodor K. Mortin	PGU (KGB)	1971–74
Vladimir A. Kryuchkov	PGU (KGB)	1974–88
Leonid V. Shebarshin	PGU (KGB)	1988–Sept. 23, 1991
Yevgeny M. Primakov	PGU (KGB)	Sept. 30–Oct. 22, 1991
	TsR	Oct. 22–Dec. 18, 1991
	SVR	Dec. 19, 1991–1996

Key:
INU Foreign Directorate
KI Committee on Information
PGU First Chief Directorate [foreign intelligence]
SVR Foreign Intelligence Service (independent)
TsR Central Intelligence Service

Appendix 4

US-Soviet Summit Meetings, 1945–91

1945	Yalta*	Stalin-Roosevelt
1945	Potsdam*	Stalin-Truman
1955	Geneva*	Khrushchev-Eisenhower
1959	Washington	Khrushchev-Eisenhower
1961	Vienna	Khrushchev-Kennedy
1967	Glassboro	Kosygin-Johnson
1972	Moscow	Brezhnev-Nixon
1973	Washington	Brezhnev-Nixon
1974	Moscow	Brezhnev-Nixon
1974	Vladivostok	Brezhnev-Ford
1979	Vienna	Brezhnev-Carter
1985	Geneva	Gorbachev-Reagan
1986	Reykjavik	Gorbachev-Reagan
1987	Washington	Gorbachev-Reagan
1988	Moscow	Gorbachev-Reagan
1988	New York	Gorbachev-Reagan
1989	Malta	Gorbachev-Bush
1990	Washington	Gorbachev-Bush
1990	Helsinki	Gorbachev-Bush
1990	Paris*	Gorbachev-Bush
1991	Madrid*	Gorbachev-Bush
1991	Moscow	Gorbachev-Bush

*These meetings involved leaders of other nations as well.

Notes

Introduction

1. Notably, see Jonathan Haslam, *Russia's Cold War: From the October Revolution to the Fall of the Wall* (New Haven, CT: Yale University Press, 2011), pp. ix, and 1–28, and the book's subtitle.
2. The most recent and thorough is Gar Alperovitz, *The Decision to Use the Atomic Bomb: And the Architecture of an American Myth* (New York: Alfred A. Knopf, 1995), updating a volume first published by Alperovitz thirty years earlier.
3. On Stalin's views on nuclear weapons in the formative years of the Cold War, the principal study is David Holloway, *Stalin and the Bomb: The Soviet Union and Atomic Strategy, 1939–1956* (New Haven, CT: Yale University Press, 1994), pp. 116–33, 225–53, and 367–70.

Chapter 1. Stalin

1. Vojtech Mastny, *The Cold War and Soviet Insecurity: The Stalin Years* (Oxford: Oxford University Press, 1996), p. 18. For extensive review of Litvinov's role in the wartime and early postwar years, see Haslam, *Russia's Cold War*, pp. 14–76. Both volumes have extensive coverage of US, UK, and USSR interactions in the wartime and early postwar years. In addition, see William Taubman, *Stalin's American Policy: From Entente to Cold War* (New York: W. W. Norton, 1982).
2. Albert Resis, ed., *Molotov Remembers: Inside Kremlin Politics* (Chicago: Ivan R. Dee, 1993), pp. 67–69; Vojtech Mastny, "The Cassandra in the Foreign Commissariat: Maxim Litvinov and the Cold War," *Foreign Affairs* 54 (Winter 1975–76): pp. 366–76; Taubman, *Stalin's American Policy*, pp. 132–33.
3. Aleksandr Feklisov, *Za okeanom i na ostrove: Zapiski razvedchika* (Beyond the ocean and on an island: Notes of an intelligence officer) (Moscow: DEM, 1994), pp. 51–52. Stalin also reaffirmed that Soviet espionage should continue to obtain information on the secret military and scientific technology of the United States, Britain, and Canada.
4. Charles E. Bohlen, *Witness to History, 1929–1969* (New York: W. W. Norton, 1973), pp. 146, 172, 180, and 217.

5. Numerous sources; see in particular Christopher Andrew and Vasili Mitrokhin, *The Sword and the Shield: The Mitrokhin Archive and the Secret History of the KGB* (New York: Basic Books, 1999), pp. 104–75. Most notable were five students at Cambridge University who turned to communism and were recruited into Soviet intelligence in the mid-1930s. They entered British government service and spied until 1951, when two who had come under suspicion fled to Moscow. Known as the "Cambridge Five," they were Anthony Blunt, Guy Burgess, John Cairncross, Donald Maclean, and Kim Philby.

6. Ibid., pp. 90 and 95; and see Genrikh Borovik, *The Philby Files: The Secret Life of Master Spy Kim Philby* (Boston: Little, Brown, 1994), pp. 198–220.

7. Andrew and Mitrokhin, *Sword and the Shield*, pp. 119–21; and Nigel West and Oleg Tsarev, *The Crown Jewels: The British Secrets at the Heart of the KGB Archives* (New Haven: Yale University Press, 1999), pp. 147–49 and 159–67. The Five were exonerated in 1944 by General Fitin and again in 1948 by another review in the wake of renewed suspicions. See West and Tsarev, *Crown Jewels*, pp. 147–67; Borovik, *Philby Files*, pp. 231–34; and Richard J. Aldrich, *The Hidden Hand: Britain, America, and Cold War Secret Intelligence* (London: John Murray, 2001), p. 442.

8. For examples, see the discussions in Andrew and Mitrokhin, *Sword and the Shield*, pp. 120–21, and Yuri Modin, *My Five Cambridge Friends: Burgess, Maclean, Philby, Blunt and Cairncross* (New York: Farrar, Straus & Giroux, 1994), p. 183.

9. Alexander Feklisov and Sergei Kostin, *The Man behind the Rosenbergs* (New York: Enigma Books, 2001), p. 67. There apparently was contingency consideration in 1942–43 with respect to the possibility of establishing a Western military presence in the Black Sea–Caucasus area in case of a Soviet military collapse there in order to counter a German advance into the Middle East. The agent in OSS was almost certainly Duncan Lee, personal assistant to OSS chief Maj. Gen. "Wild Bill" Donovan.

10. Aldrich, *Hidden Hand*, pp. 57–59 (and see pp. 44–63 and 107–18), and Joint Planning Staff, "Operation 'Unthinkable,'" May 25, 1945, Churchill to Ismay, June 10, 1945, CAB 120/691, UK National Archives, Kew.

11. See [Col.] O. A. Rzheshevskii, "Churchill's Secret War Plans against the USSR in May 1945," *Novaya i noveishaya istoriya* (Modern and contemporary history), no. 3 (June 1999): pp. 98–123, and [Col.] Oleg I. Tsarev, "The USSR and England: From Cooperation to Confrontation

(1941–1945)," *Novaya i noveishaya istoriya*, no. 1 (January/February 1998): pp. 92–105; "Secret Mission 'Nord,' Churchill's Secret Weapon," *Voyenno-istoricheskii zhurnal* (The military-historical journal), nos. 6, 7, and 8 (June, July, and August 1993); Vladislav Zubok, *A Failed Empire: The Soviet Union in the Cold War from Stalin to Gorbachev* (Chapel Hill: University of North Carolina Press, 2007), p. 16; and Oleg Tsarev, "Soviet Intelligence on British Defence Plans 1945–1950," in *Intelligence in the Cold War*, ed. Lars C. Jenssen and Olav Riste (Oslo: Norwegian Institute for Defense Studies, 2001), pp. 53–56.

12. Col. Gen. S. N. Lebedev, chief ed., *Ocherki istorii Rossiiskoi vneshnei razvedki* (Essays on the history of Russian foreign intelligence), vol. 5 (Moscow: Mezhdunarodniye Otnosheniya,2003), p. 35, citing JCS 1496/2.

13. See Anthony Cave Brown, ed., *Dropshot: The United States Plan for War with the Soviet Union in 1957* (New York: Dial Press, 1978). In addition to the text of Dropshot, Brown's book contains commentary and discussion of other US war plans of 1945–50. See also Steven T. Ross, *American War Plans 1945–1950: Strategies for Defeating the Soviet Union* (London: Frank Cass, 1996); Gregg Herken, *The Winning Weapon: The Atomic Bomb in the Cold War 1945–1950* (New York: Alfred A. Knopf, 1980); and Thomas H. Etzold and John Lewis Gaddis, *Containment: Documents on American Policy and Strategy, 1945–1950* (New York: Columbia University Press, 1978), including the text of NSC-68, which was titled United States Objectives and Programs for National Security, April 14, 1950.

14. The official *Ocherki istorii Rossiiskoi vneshnei razvedki*, vol. 5, 2003, pp. 35–42, and vol. 6, 2005, p. 7, reviews these US war plans in some detail but without stating when they became known to Soviet intelligence, except for a suspiciously vague claim that they had been acquired in a "timely" way. Also see Maj. Gen. Yury Drozdov, "The Best Friend of Dictator [Alfredo] Stroessner," *Izvestiya*, April 17, 1999. Drozdov notes that two well-placed clandestine Soviet spies operating in Latin America were given an assignment in 1955 to obtain the Dropshot war plan but were—not surprisingly—unable to do so in five years of effort.

15. For a review of such Soviet military commentaries, see Raymond L. Garthoff, "Soviet Perceptions of Western Strategic Thought and Doctrine," in *Soviet Military Doctrine and Western Policy*, ed. Gregory Flynn (London: Routledge, 1989), pp. 197–327, esp. pp. 220–26. When NSC-68 was declassified in 1975 and shown to the Soviet General Staff, it was regarded with amazement for postulating possible multiple offensives

by Soviet armed forces in the early 1950s, far exceeding what was realistic. See Georgy M. Kornienko, *Kholodnaya Voina: Svidetel'stvo eë uchastnika* (The Cold War: Testimony of a participant) (Moscow: Mezhdunarodniye Otnosheniya, 1994), p. 36.

16. Feklisov, *Za okeanom*, pp. 118–19, 123, 138–39; and Feklisov and Kostin, *Man behind Rosenbergs*, pp. 187–88 and 338. The objectives stated in the JCS contingency war plans always gave priority to the two objectives of repulsing Soviet forces invading Western Europe and the Middle East and destroying the war-making capabilities of the USSR, but they also sought (as, for example, in the 1948 war plan Charioteer) "to compel the withdrawal of Soviet military and political forces from areas under their control or domination [to] within 1939 borders," "abandonment of any ideology which advocates world domination," and "the creation of governments [note the plural]" that would "practice goodwill toward all nations." Cited in Brown, *Dropshot*, p. 6.

17. Pavel Sudoplatov and Anatoli Sudoplatov, with Jerrold L. and Leona P. Schecter, *Special Tasks: The Memoirs of an Unwanted Witness—A Soviet Spymaster* (Boston: Little, Brown, 1994), p. 210. As of July 1946 the United States had only nine atomic bombs, and they were kept in a disassembled state.

18. For two studies based mainly on declassified American documentary records, see Peter Grose, *Operation Rollback: America's Secret War behind the Iron Curtain* (Boston: Houghton Mifflin, 2000), and Gregory Mitrovich, *Undermining the Kremlin: America's Strategy to Subvert the Soviet Bloc, 1947–1956* (Ithaca, NY: Cornell University Press, 2000). There are also useful additional accounts in many memoirs by former CIA officials. On British clandestine operations in the Baltic states, see Tom Bower, *The Red Web: MI6 and the KGB Master Coup* (London: Aurum, 1989). On US use of the European Recovery Program, or Marshall Plan, to finance such operations, see Sally Pisani, *The CIA and the Marshall Plan* (Edinburgh: Edinburgh University Press, 1991). For the impact on Soviet intelligence assessments, see General of the Army Filipp D. Bobkov, *KGB i vlast'* (The KGB and state authority) (Moscow: Veteran MP, 1995), pp. 43–57, and Christopher Andrew and Oleg Gordievsky, *KGB: The Inside Story of Its Foreign Operations from Lenin to Gorbachev* (New York: HarperCollins, 1990), pp. 384–90. The most effective Western efforts aimed at subversion were the broadcasts of radio stations such as Radio Free Europe.

19. For an excellent analysis of Stalin's speech and the general development of the early Cold War, see Albert Resis, *Stalin, the Politburo, and the*

Onset of the Cold War, 1945–1946, Carl Beck Papers, no. 701 (Pittsburgh, PA: University of Pittsburgh Center for Russian and East European Studies, 1988).

20. Archives of the International Information Department (OMI) and the Foreign Policy Department (OVP) of the Communist Party Central Committee showed a clear change during 1946 in intelligence reports and analyses to finding the United States to be dominant in Western policy in the Middle East, in place of Britain. See N. I. Yegorova, "The Iran Crisis, 1945–1946: As Seen from the Russian Archives," in *Kholodnaya voina: Novye podkhody, novye dokumenty* (The Cold War: New approaches, new documents) (Moscow: Institute of Universal History, Russian Academy of Sciences, 1995), p. 310.

21. Some Russian historians have described that speech as virtually a Western declaration of cold war. Most Western historians, including this author, see it rather as reflecting Churchill's recognition of the existence of a cold war caused by the Soviet decision to impose its control over Eastern Europe and to gear up for global confrontation with the West. As is evident in this example, contending perceptions based on reciprocated views of the other side as an adversary initiating confrontation marked both the Cold War and retrospective analyses attempting to understand it better in historical perspective.

22. Kennan's telegram (no. 408, February 22, 1946) is reproduced in *Foreign Relations of the United States, 1946*, vol. 6 (1969), pp. 696–709. A July 1947 *Foreign Affairs* article by "X" (Kennan) based on it energized US public opinion in support of waging the Cold War. Together they recommended a Western policy aimed at "containment" of Soviet expansionist tendencies until Soviet ideological conceptions atrophied.

23. The Novikov document was first presented to a joint US-Soviet conference of historians in June 1990, and Ambassador Vladimir Shustov drew the parallel between it and Kennan's telegram. This led American participants to misunderstand that the Novikov document also had been a telegram. See Kenneth M. Jensen, ed., *Origins of the Cold War: The Novikov, Kennan, and Roberts "Long Telegrams" of 1946*, rev. ed. (Washington: United States Institute of Peace, 1993), which erroneously identifies the analysis as a telegram sent from Novikov in Washington to Molotov in Moscow on September 24, 1946 (both were then in Paris at the peace treaty negotiations). The archival copy of the briefing released includes Molotov's marginal notations, providing an interesting direct indication of his views on a number of points discussed in the document, a draft of which he had discussed with Novikov.

The Novikov paper was later published in the official Soviet journal *Mezhdunarodnaya zhizn'* (International affairs), November, 1990. See also Nikolai V. Novikov, *Vospominaniya diplomata: Zapiski 1938–1947* (Recollections of a diplomat: Notes from 1938–1947) (Moscow: Politizdat, 1989), pp. 352–53.

24. Jensen, *Origins of the Cold War*, p. 3. Here, and in later cited excerpts, the passages in italics were underlined by Molotov. The emphasized phrase here could alternatively be translated as "world domination."

25. Ibid., pp. 7 and 15–16.

26. See Mastny, *Cold War and Soviet Insecurity*, pp. 27–29; Zubok, *Failed Empire*, pp. 72–73; Scott D. Parrish and Mikhail M. Narinsky, *New Evidence on the Soviet Rejection of the Marshall Plan, 1947: Two Reports*, Working Paper No. 9, Cold War International History Project (Washington: Woodrow Wilson International Center for Scholars, 1994), esp. p. 45; Vladimir Pechatnov, *The Big Three after World War II: New Documents on Soviet Thinking about Post War Relations with the United States and Great Britain*, Working Paper No. 13, Cold War International History Project (Washington: Woodrow Wilson International Center for Scholars, 1995); Vladislav Zubok and Constantine Pleshakov, *Inside the Kremlin's Cold War: From Stalin to Khrushchev* (Cambridge, MA: Harvard University Press, 1996), pp. 103–8; and Sudoplatov and Sudoplatov, *Special Tasks*, pp. 230–32.

27. The attack on Novikov and his 1946 analysis by his own embassy deputy is now declassified in the Foreign Ministry archives. It is cited by Zubok and Pleshakov, *Inside the Kremlin's Cold War*, pp. 103–4, and had earlier been referred to in Viktor L. Mal'kov, "Commentary," in *Diplomatic History* 15, no. 4 (Fall 1991): pp. 556–57. Tarasenko's denunciation was (unusually) distributed to all Politburo members. The attack, given Molotov's sponsorship of Novikov's analysis, is intriguing. Moreover, Molotov had discussed with Novikov and endorsed an analysis of the Truman Doctrine and Marshall Plan that Novikov had prepared in August 1947. (See Novikov, *Vospominaniya diplomata*, pp. 379, 391, and 394–96, and Holloway, *Stalin and the Bomb*, p. 255.) Molotov did not defend Novikov, but he did cushion his downfall by permitting him to resign from the diplomatic service rather than suffer more dire consequences.

28. See Andrew and Mitrokhin, *Sword and the Shield*, p. 54.

29. See "Answers of the Chief of the Group of Consultants of the Foreign Intelligence Service of Russia, Lt. General V. V. Kirpichenko, to Questions from the Journal 'Modern and Contemporary History,'" *Novaya*

i noveishaya istoriya (Modern and contemporary history), no. 4 (July/August 1997): pp. 87–88.

30. Stalin's reported remark is cited in an excellent discussion by Christopher Andrew and Julie Elkner, "Stalin and Foreign Intelligence," *Totalitarian Movements and Political Religions* 4, no. 1 (2010): p. 75.

31. An information and analysis body, the Information Service (SI), was created after the security and intelligence organs were constituted as a People's Commissariat for State Security (the NKGB) separate from the Commissariat for Internal Affairs (the NKVD), in April 1943. In March 1946 the NKGB became a ministry (the MGB), and the SI was raised in status to become the Information Directorate of the MGB. After the dissolution of the Communist International (Comintern) in May 1943, its international intelligence analysis and reports section was moved under the Central Committee of the Communist Party in July 1944 as the International Information Department (OMI). In December 1945 a Foreign Policy Department (OVP) of the Central Committee was also established.

32. *Foreign Relations of the United States, 1946*, vol. 6 (1969), Telegram No. 408 (February 22, 1946) p. 707; and Telegram No. 878 (March 20, 1946), p. 722.

33. For an authoritative summary of the KI, see D. P. Prokhorov, *Razvedka ot Stalina do Putina* (Intelligence from Stalin to Putin) (Saint-Petersburg: Dom Neva, 2004), pp. 241–49; and see Andrew and Mitrokhin, *Sword and the Shield*, pp. 144–46. Panyushkin had long served in Soviet intelligence prior to his posting as ambassador to the United States, and soon after returning to Moscow he became the chief of the foreign intelligence service (from 1953 to 1955).

34. The Small KI archives, which have been declassified, are held by the Foreign Ministry. I have read a number of the KI reports and can attest to their overall quality. A more complete study of the Small KI reports for 1952–53, including the Iranian case, is to be found in Vladislav Zubok, "Soviet Intelligence and the Cold War: The 'Small' Committee of Information, 1952–53," *Diplomatic History* 19, no. 3 (Summer 1995): pp. 453–72 (on Iran, pp. 466–68).

35. A purge of Soviet intelligence officers cost their services expertise, and the defections of Igor Guzenko in Canada and Elizabeth Bentley in the United States in the fall of 1945 caused the withdrawal or extended deactivation of most Soviet intelligence officers in North America. Virtually the only major Soviet espionage success in the United States in the earliest years of the Cold War was learning that the United States had

broken Soviet intelligence codes, an achievement based on information obtained by William Weisband, an agent recruited much earlier. Weisband's reporting of this important information was, however, delayed for two years because his contact with Soviet intelligence had been cut off from early 1946 to late 1948. See Andrew and Mitrokhin, *Sword and the Shield*, pp. 144 and 155–56, and John Earl Haynes, Harvey Klehr and Alexander Vassiliev, *Spies: The Rise and Fall of the KGB in America* (New Haven: Yale University Press, 2009), pp. 398–405. Indeed, the only significant Soviet intelligence access to US policymaking in this period came through three members of the Cambridge Five: Philby, as SIS representative in Washington from 1949 to 1951, Burgess at the British Embassy in Washington during 1950–51, and Maclean as head of the American desk at the Foreign Office in London, also in 1950–51.

36. Andrew and Mitrokhin, *Sword and the Shield*, pp. 150–54.

37. Amy Knight, *How the Cold War Began: The Igor Gouzenko Affair and the Hunt for Soviet Spies* (New York: Carroll & Graf, 2005), p. 100, and see pp. 169–72 on continuing use by the MGB of the Guzenko case to denigrate the rival GRU military intelligence service. On the suspension of most espionage in North America, see also Andrew and Mitrokhin, *Sword and the Shield*, pp. 47–51; Andrew and Gordievsky, *KGB*, pp. 367–75; Allen Weinstein and Alexander Vassiliev, *The Haunted Wood: Soviet Espionage in America—The Stalin Era* (New York: Random House, 1999), pp. 104–7; and Haynes et al., *Spies*, pp. 518–33.

38. Lt. Gen. Sergei Kondrashev in David E. Murphy, Sergei A. Kondrashev, and George Bailey, *Battleground Berlin: CIA vs. KGB in the Cold War* (New Haven: Yale University Press, 1997), p. 42.

39. See Aleksandr Sever, *Istoriya KGB* (A history of the KGB) (Moscow: Algoritm, 2008), p. 13; and Lt. Gen. Leonid V. Shebarshin, *Ruka Moskvy: Zapiski nachal'nika sovetskoi razvedki* (The arm of Moscow: Notes of the chief of Soviet intelligence) (Moscow: Tsentr-100, 1992), pp. 150–52.

40. A. A. Gromyko et al., eds., *Istoriya diplomatii* (The history of diplomacy), 2nd ed., vol. 5, book 2 (Moscow: Politizdat, 1979), p. 745. Gromyko's own diplomatic record, while impressive, was spotty on objectivity, and his memoir is far from objective.

41. After Stalin's death, Beria as one of the new collective leadership succeeding Stalin was made head of a newly combined intelligence and security body, the MVD (Ministry of Internal Affairs), but he was arrested only three months later and subsequently executed. Beria had sent some of his own security officers into East Germany during debate among the leaders over policy toward Germany, raising concern among

them. His successor was a professional security officer, Col. Gen. Sergei Kruglov, not a political figure.

Chapter 2. Khrushchev

1. Zubok and Pleshakov, *Inside the Kremlin's Cold War*, p. 157.
2. Two days after Eisenhower's speech, which John Foster Dulles had not favored, Dulles followed it with a vintage "Cold War speech" championing the liberation theme rather than encouraging possible change in the Soviet Union. For background, see Raymond L. Garthoff, *Assessing the Adversary: Estimates by the Eisenhower Administration of Soviet Intentions and Capabilities* (Washington: Brookings Institution, 1991), pp. 6–8. The KI, however, instead of recognizing that Dulles was taking a harder line than Eisenhower, concluded that the stiff Dulles diatribe was intended to reinforce the Eisenhower speech rather than to undercut it. See Zubok, "Soviet Intelligence and the Cold War," p. 461.
3. "Speech of G. M. Malenkov," *Izvestiya*, August 9, 1953.
4. See "Speech of G. M. Malenkov," *Pravda*, March 13, 1954, and "Speech of A. I. Mikoyan," *Kommunist* (Yerevan), March 12, 1954. Malenkov's speech was almost certainly prompted by a sobering account of future thermonuclear bombs and a real threat to world civilization prepared by Academician Igor Kurchatov, head of the Soviet nuclear weapons program, and discussed with Malenkov before it was officially submitted to him, Molotov, and Khrushchev on April 1, 1954, by Kurchatov's superior, Deputy Premier Vyacheslav Malyshev. Malenkov thus jumped the gun on a public recognition of this impending revolution in political-military affairs without adequate consideration of how his rivals, Khrushchev and Molotov, could and would use his daring initiative against him. Khrushchev completely embraced the Malenkov line after securing power, and Molotov was excluded from the leadership for continuing to hold Stalinist views on this and other matters. See Zubok, *Failed Empire*, pp. 124–27, on the Kurchatov memorandum.
5. I. V. Stalin, "Economic Problems of Socialism in the USSR," *Bol'shevik*, no. 18 (September 1952): pp. 18–19.
6. For a more complete analysis, see Raymond L. Garthoff, "The Death of Stalin and the Birth of Mutual Deterrence," *Survey* (London) 25, no. 2 (Spring 1980): pp. 10–16.
7. As late as the Moscow summit meeting of June 1988, Ronald Reagan reluctantly rejected a communiqué reference to "peaceful coexistence" proposed by Mikhail Gorbachev, after George Shultz and Frank

Carlucci persuaded him to withdraw his initial readiness to include it. See Igor Korchilov, *Translating History: Thirty Years on the Front Lines of Diplomacy with a Top Russian Interpreter* (New York: Scribner, 1997), pp. 177–80.

8. Nikita Khrushchev, *Khrushchev Remembers*, ed. and trans. Strobe Talbott (Boston: Little, Brown, 1970), p. 400.

9. Bohlen, *Witness to History*, p. 389.

10. Zubok, *Failed Empire*, p. 107. The "Open Skies" proposal by President Eisenhower would have required exchanges of military information and reciprocal overflights by the United States and the USSR of the territory of the other to verify this military information. It was promptly rejected. See Garthoff, *Assessing the Adversary*, pp. 10–12.

11. See Aleksandr Fursenko and Timothy Naftali, *Khrushchev's Cold War: The Inside Story of an American Adversary* (New York: W. W. Norton, 2006), pp. 99–137.

12. Ibid., p. 130. See also Sergei Khrushchev, *Nikita Khrushchev and the Creation of a Superpower* (University Park: Penn State University Press, 2000), p. 211; William Taubman, *Khrushchev: The Man and His Era* (New York: W. W. Norton, 2003), pp. 359–60; and Zubok and Pleshakov, *Inside the Kremlin's Cold War*, p. 191.

13. In August 1957, I personally visited the Ministry of Defense in Moscow and sought an interview with Marshal Zhukov. Two days later, I was called in by the colonel to whom I had given my request and got an answer. "The Marshal," he said, "has read your book [*Soviet Military Doctrine* (Glencoe, IL: Free Press, 1953)] and would very much have liked to talk to you but regrettably cannot do so in view of the press of his duties, military and political" (emphasis added). I was not surprised that Zhukov did not receive me, but I did find it interesting that even in such a minor matter he would not only respond to an unofficial approach by an American but also that he would go out of his way to emphasize his political role.

14. Georgy Kornienko, later first deputy foreign minister, serving in 1958 in the newly established Information (Evaluation) Service of the Central Committee (successor to the Small KI) headed by Ambassador Georgy Pushkin, informed me that he believed the inspiration for Khrushchev's initiative on Berlin stemmed at least in part from the fact that Pushkin had drawn Khrushchev's attention to a speech by Secretary of State John Foster Dulles in October 1958 comparing the importance of Quemoy to West Berlin and that thinking about that may have led Khrushchev to decide to push on Berlin. Paradoxically, Pushkin, a

former ambassador to East Germany, argued strongly against any attempt to force the West out of Berlin.

15. See Memorandum of Conversation, "Mikoyan's Call on the President," January 17, 1959, p. 6.

16. An extensive summary of the annual report by the chairman of the KGB to Khrushchev on 1960, submitted on February 14, 1961, is provided in Vladislav M. Zubok, "Spy vs. Spy: The KGB vs. the CIA, 1960–1962," *Cold War International History Project Bulletin*, no. 4 (Fall 1994): pp. 22–24.

17. For an analysis of American assessment and policy in the Khrushchev period, see Garthoff, *Assessing the Adversary*.

18. See Fursenko and Naftali, *Khrushchev's Cold War*, pp. 339–40.

19. See Raymond L. Garthoff, *A Journey through the Cold War: A Memoir of Containment and Coexistence* (Washington: Brookings Institution, 2001), pp. 132–38; Michael Beschloss, *The Crisis Years: Kennedy and Khrushchev, 1960–1963* (New York: Edward Burlingame Books / HarperCollins, 1991), pp. 60–61; and Christopher Andrew and Vasili Mitrokhin, *The World Was Going Our Way: The KGB and the Battle for the Third World* (New York: Basic Books, 2005), pp. 9–10.

20. See Fursenko and Naftali, *Khrushchev's Cold War*, pp. 348–49.

21. See ibid., pp. 341, 349–50, 403–4, 418–20, 462–63, and 530; and see academician A. A. Fursenko, "The Unusual Fate of Intelligence Officer G. N. Bol'shakov," *Novaya i noveishaya istoriya* (Modern and contemporary history), no. 4 (July/August 2005), pp. 92–101.

22. See Fursenko and Naftali, *Khrushchev's Cold War*, pp. 372–74, and Andrew and Gordievsky, KGB, pp. 460–62.

23. See Khrushchev, *Nikita Khrushchev and the Creation of a Superpower*, p. 535.

24. See Fursenko, "Unusual Fate of Intelligence Officer," p. 94, citing the archives of the Russian Foreign Intelligence Service (Sluzhba Vneshnei Razvedki, or SVR) but with no precise reference. Andrew and Mitrokhin, *Sword and the Shield*, p. 180, also discusses this report and states that the "collaborator" was a Western European NATO liaison officer with the CIA.

25. Fursenko, "Unusual Fate of Intelligence Officer," pp. 94–95.

26. Fursenko and Naftali, *Khrushchev's Cold War*, p. 424. A more far-reaching version of this GRU report appears in Andrew and Mitrokhin, *Sword and the Shield*, p. 182, without indication of its source. The latter account states that a decision to launch a nuclear attack had been made in June but canceled in September after the nuclear test. Such

a decision, however, on its face is not credible: If a decision to attack had been made, or even if one were under consideration, indications of advances in nuclear tests (which could not be weaponized for a considerable time) would only have reinforced arguments for a preventive strike and not led to reversing such a decision or dropping one under consideration.

27. Fursenko and Naftali, *Khrushchev's Cold War*, pp. 396 and 427.

28. Ibid., pp. 412–16.

29. For a more full account and sourcing, see Raymond L. Garthoff, "The American-Soviet Tank Confrontation at Checkpoint Charlie," in *Mysteries of the Cold War*, ed. Steven J. Cimbala (Aldershot: Ashgate, 1999), pp. 73–87.

30. Khrushchev, *Khrushchev Remembers*, pp. 459–60.

31. For discussion of this problem with respect to the Berlin contingency military planning in 1961, see Garthoff, *Journey through the Cold War*, pp. 127–31.

32. For a brief review of some such penetrations in 1961, including the findings of NATO (and American) "damage assessments" of a case in 1968 in which the author participated, and other evidence, see Garthoff, *Journey through the Cold War*, pp. 234–35. The United States sometimes passed secret information to NATO knowing that it would probably be acquired by Soviet and other Warsaw Pact intelligence agents, in cases where it wanted such information to go to Moscow and knew that the Soviet leaders often gave greater credence to information received from clandestine intelligence than from open sources. This was done because the United States wanted them to know in certain cases how much it knew about some of their activities and sometimes to let them know what the United States was planning or was prepared to do if necessary.

33. For a detailed account, see ibid., pp. 114–16. The author sought to have this information declassified, but that did not happen until after the end of the Cold War.

34. See Raymond L. Garthoff, *Soviet Military Policy: A Historical Analysis* (New York: Frederick A. Praeger, 1966), pp. 65–97 and 191–237, for the ideological foundation for this pragmatic conclusion.

35. Fursenko and Naftali, *Khrushchev's Cold War*, p. 420. See also Beschloss, *Crisis Years*, pp. 345–47 and 362.

36. Ibid., pp. 427–39, and see 443–507.

37. For an analytical summary of the Cuban Missile Crisis, see Garthoff, *Journey through the Cold War*, pp. 168–87. For the best overall account,

see Michael Dobbs, *One Minute to Midnight: Kennedy, Khrushchev, and Castro on the Brink of Nuclear War* (New York: Alfred A. Knopf, 2008). Khrushchev's misadventure was scathingly criticized by the Chinese communists as both "adventurism" for deploying strategic missiles in Cuba and then "capitulationism" for taking them out.

38. On this general subject, see James G. Blight and David A. Welch, eds., *Intelligence and the Cuban Missile Crisis* (London: Frank Cass, 1999), especially the chapters on Soviet intelligence by Aleksandr Fursenko and Timothy Naftali, pp. 64–87, and on US intelligence by Raymond L. Garthoff, pp. 18–63.

39. Nikita Khrushchev, *Khrushchev Remembers: The Glasnost Tapes*, ed. and trans. Jerrold Schecter and Vyacheslav V. Luchkov (Boston: Little, Brown, 1990), p. 80.

40. Ibid., p. 180. The reference from the personal letter is cited by his son Sergei Khrushchev in *Nikita Khrushchev and the Creation of a Superpower*, p. 641.

41. "Toward a Strategy of Peace: Address by President Kennedy," June 10, 1963, in *Department of State Bulletin* 49, no. 1253 (July 1, 1963): pp. 2–6.

42. Regrettably, a comprehensive nuclear test ban eluded agreement, owing to a misunderstanding in informal discussions from which Khrushchev understood three on-site inspections per year to monitor an agreement would be acceptable, while the US position called for a minimum of seven, and both leaders had stretched to come even that close.

43. For discussion of these measures, see Garthoff, *Journey through the Cold War*, pp. 154–67.

44. Fursenko and Naftali, *Khrushchev's Cold War*, p. 530. They report that the KGB tried to find evidence to support this belief but without success—but also without excluding it.

Chapter 3. Brezhnev

1. See Raymond L. Garthoff, *Détente and Confrontation: American-Soviet Relations from Nixon to Reagan*, rev. ed. (Washington: Brookings Institution, 1994), pp. 40–73.

2. Khrushchev strongly opposed Soviet involvement in local or limited wars, while the military and its military-industrial allies believed they should build up all aspects of military power to deter, if not to fight, the whole range of possible military actions. In a key Defense Council meeting in March 1963 with the military leadership, Khrushchev lost all

support when he made clear his intention to cut back all the armed services and pursue only a limited expansion of the strategic missile forces. See Sergei Khrushchev, cited in Taubman, *Khrushchev*, pp. 263–72.

3. See Raymond L. Garthoff, "The Aborted US-USSR Summit of 1965," *SHAFR* [Society for Historians of American Foreign Relations] *Newsletter* 32, no. 2 (June 2001): pp. 1–2.

4. Georgy Arbatov, *The System: An Insider's Life in Soviet Politics* (New York: Times Books, 1992), pp. 172–74.

5. Andrew and Mitrokhin, *Sword and the Shield*, pp. 203–4.

6. For 1939 and 1946, see Feklisov and Kostin, *Man behind the Rosenbergs*, pp. 413 and 164; for the figures for 1941–43, see Lt. Gen. Vadim Kirpichenko, *Razvedka: Litsa i lichnosti* (Intelligence: Its features and personalities) (Moscow: Geya, 1998), p. 235; for the estimates for the mid-1960s and mid-1980s, presumably by Gordievsky, see Christopher Andrew and Oleg Gordievsky, *Comrade Khrushchev's Instructions: Top Secret Files on KGB Foreign Operations, 1975–1985* (Stanford, CA: Stanford University Press, 1993), p. xiii. Oleg Kalugin, *The First Directorate: My 32 Years in Intelligence and Espionage against the West* (New York: St. Martin's Press, 1994), p. 149, estimates twelve thousand in the mid-1970s. For the last half of the 1980s, see Prokhorov, *Razvedka ot Stalina do Putina*, p. 108. For comparison, the GRU probably numbered about fifteen thousand by 1990, and it was reduced in 1992 to eleven thousand; p. 233.

7. Nikolai S. Leonov, *Likholet'ye: Sekretnye missii* (The troubled years: Secret missions) (Moscow: Mezhdunarodniye Otnosheniya, 1995), p. 129.

8. Most of this information comes from multiple sources; General Leonov's memoir provides the most complete rundown, ibid., especially pp. 121–33. The comments on reporting from the New York residency are from Arkady N. Shevchenko, *Breaking with Moscow* (New York: Alfred A. Knopf, 1985), pp. 206–7.

9. On the development of Soviet-Chinese relations, in particular from 1969 to 1972, see Garthoff, *Détente and Confrontation*, pp. 228–42 and 719, including the Richardson reference; also see Shevchenko, Breaking with Moscow, pp. 164–68, including the reference to Dobrynin's report to Moscow; Leonov, *Likholet'ye*, p. 147, on divided KGB views; and on the possibility that it was ill-conceived disinformation, see Andrew and Gordievsky, *KGB*, p. 494.

10. See Andrew and Gordievsky, *Comrade Kryuchkov's Instructions*, p. 2; and confirmation from other Soviet intelligence officers.

11. Leonov, *Likholet'ye*, p. 147.

12. See Shevchenko, *Breaking with Moscow*, pp. 200–1. Shevchenko was at the time a close adviser to Gromyko.

13. "Open Letter of the CPSU to the CCP," *Pravda*, July 14, 1963. The Soviet firm assertion of peaceful coexistence carried over into the authoritative declarations of the CPSU Congresses of 1966 and 1971, where it bolstered Soviet support for détente with the West.

14. See Garthoff, *Détente and Confrontation*, pp. 279–322 and 394, and Shevchenko, *Breaking with Moscow*, pp. 212–16.

15. Leonov, *Likholet'ye*, pp. 162–63.

16. See Prokhorov, *Razvedka ot Stalina do Putina*, pp. 397–402; Kalugin, *First Directorate*, pp. 151–53; and Kalugin, *Proshchai Lubyanka!* (Farewell, Lubyanka!) (Moscow: Olymp, 1995), pp. 167–71.

17. See Raymond L. Garthoff, "New Evidence on Soviet Intelligence: The KGB's 1967 Annual Report," *Cold War International History Project Bulletin*, no. 10 (March 1998), p. 212.

18. See Kalugin, *Proshchai Lubyanka!*, pp. 172–74.

19. Kalugin, *First Directorate*, p. 108.

20. Kirpichenko, *Razvedka*, pp. 32–33. Emphasis added.

21. Volkogonov, *Sem' vozhdei*, pp. 99–101, 87–89, and 130–33, based on Volkogonov's review of the archival files.

22. Peak American annual production of tanks during World War II was 50,000. In making the 1974 estimate, no allowance was made for factors such as the greater complexity of modern tanks or competing resource demands—to say nothing about the wartime vulnerability of production facilities. In 1974 the United States had 8,226 tanks, 5,049 of which were modern main battle tanks, with one factory producing tanks and an annual wartime production capability of 500–600 tanks.

23. Vitaly Shlykov, "Chto pogubilo Sovetskii Soyuz? Genshtab i ekonomika" (What destroyed the Soviet Union? The General Staff and the economy), *Voennyi vestnik*, no. 9 (September 2002), supplement, pp. 118–20; and Vitaly Shlykov, "Fatal Mistakes of the US and Soviet Intelligence: Part One," *International Affairs* (Moscow) 43, no. 1 (January 1997): pp. 171–75. Colonel Shlykov, a senior military intelligence analyst, became increasingly frustrated in his attempts to introduce more realism into GRU reporting and analysis during the 1970s and 1980s.

24. Kirpichenko, *Razvedka*, p. 340.

25. Andrew and Gordievsky, *KGB*, p. 540.

26. Ibid., pp. 540–41.

27. Lt. Gen. Leonid V. Shebarshin, *Iz zhizni nachalnika razvedki* (From the life of a chief of intelligence) (Moscow: Mezhdunarodniye Otnosheniya, 1994), p. 180.

28. See Shebarshin, *Iz zhizni*, pp. 61–62. See also Andrew and Mitrokhin, *World Was Going Our Way*, pp. 17–19; Andrew and Gordievsky, *Comrade Kryuchkov's Instructions*, pp. 91–106 and 129–39; and Christopher Andrew and Oleg Gordievsky, *More Instructions from the Centre: Top Secret Files on KGB Global Operations, 1975–1985* (London: Frank Cass, 1992), pp. 30–36, for examples from the late 1970s and early 1980s.

29. Interview with Lt. Gen. Vadim Kirpichenko, *Vremya novosti* (The day's news), Moscow, December 20, 2004.

30. Kalugin, *Proshchai Lubyanka!*, p. 131.

31. Shevchenko, *Breaking with Moscow*, pp. 160 and 244. This included intelligence provided by the KGB addressed only to Gromyko.

32. See Anatoly Dobrynin, *In Confidence: Moscow's Ambassador to America's Six Cold War Presidents (1962–1986)* (New York: Random House / Times Books, 1995); and see Shevchenko, *Breaking with Moscow*, pp. 193–98 and 256–62. The Department of State has published a unique volume that records the exchanges between Henry Kissinger and Anatoly Dobrynin as reported by each of them at the time. Now declassified by both countries, it provides not only the substance of the exchanges but also how they were perceived and reported to the leaders of both countries. See *Soviet-American Relations: The Détente Years, 1969–1972* (Washington: Government Printing Office, 2007).

33. Grechko even went so far as to suggest that Georgy Kornienko, a deputy foreign minister, had to be an American agent because of the way he pushed for a strategic arms agreement. Andropov had to assure Grechko that he was not. See Sergei F. Akhromeyev and Georgy M. Kornienko, *Glazami marshala i diplomata* (Through the eyes of a marshal and a diplomat) (Moscow: Mezhdunarodniye Otnosheniya, 1992), p. 41.

34. For the movement to East-West détente in the late 1960s and early 1970s, see the relevant chapters in Garthoff, *Détente and Confrontation*, particularly pp. 27–223.

35. Ibid., p. 343. By 1971 Brezhnev was clearly the leading figure although officially he was but one of a triumvirate of leaders (along with Prime Minister Aleksei Kosygin and President Nikolai Podgorny—all three of whom issued the invitation to President Nixon to the 1972 Moscow summit meeting). By 1973 and the Washington summit, Brezhnev was clearly the leader. Later he succeeded Podgorny (ousted in 1977) in his nominal leadership position as well. Brezhnev, however, was

increasingly limited by weak health after a stroke and heart attack in late 1974.

36. "On the Results of the Soviet-American Talks," *Pravda*, June 2, 1972. Brezhnev told Nixon and Kissinger that he considered the basic principles agreement "even more important" than the strategic arms limitation agreements reached at the meeting, to the puzzlement of both Nixon and Kissinger. See Henry A. Kissinger, *White House Years* (New York: Little, Brown, 1979), p. 1208.

37. Central Committee Archive TsKhSD, Fond 4, Opis 22, Delo 937, Letter of the CC CPSU ST 43, (archive) p. 115; (letter) p. 25. Emphasis added.

38. In post–Cold War evaluations, General Kryuchkov continued to cite the "positive role" of the Helsinki Accord in improving relations in Europe and the world, while his former chief of analysis, General Leonov, saw it as a "disaster" for the Soviet Union because it raised the issue of human rights in an international agreement. See Gen. Vladimir Kryuchkov, *Lichnoye delo* (A personal account), vol. 1 (Moscow: Olymp, 1996), p. 100, and Leonov, *Likholet'ye*, pp. 163–65.

39. See Dobrynin, *In Confidence*, pp. 218–19.

Chapter 4. Brezhnev, Andropov

1. General Leonov judged 1975 to be the high point of the Soviet state, with a gradual decline sharpened in 1979–80 by events in Afghanistan and Poland. See Leonov, *Likholet'ye*, pp. 134 and 201.

2. For an analysis of Soviet Third World military involvements in the 1975–79 period, see Garthoff, *Détente and Confrontation*, pp. 556–93 and 686–757. The overall modest scale and role of distant Soviet military presence, mainly military advisers and technical arms support personnel, is clearly shown by the now declassified detailed figures showing that the total of Soviet military deaths in the Third World from 1962 through 1979 (pre-Afghanistan) had been only 145. Ibid., p. 753.

3. Zbigniew Brzezinski, the primary exponent of a tilt in US relations with China in order to bolster confronting the Soviet Union, in his memoir describes in detail his successful campaign in 1977–80 to reverse President Carter's initial preference for even-handed relations with China and the Soviet Union. See Zbigniew Brzezinski, *Power and Principle: Memoirs of the National Security Adviser, 1977–1981* (New York: Farrar, Straus, Giroux, 1983), pp. 196–233 and 403–25.

4. Garthoff, *Détente and Confrontation*, pp. 1100 and 1101, citing both sources.

5. Some seven months later, after the Soviet invasion of Afghanistan,

Carter made some highly critical remarks about the Soviet leaders, which senior Soviet officials regarded as breaking for the first time a 1965 agreement that neither side would impugn personally the leaders of the other side. Carter was not aware of this informal understanding. See ibid., pp. 809 and 1105.

6. Ibid., pp. 910–34. See also Odd Arne Westad, ed., *The Fall of Détente: Soviet-American Relations during the Carter Years* (Oslo: Scandinavian University Press, 1997), pp. 109 and 281–85. Indeed, according to Paul Nitze's biographer (and grandson), Nitze deliberately encouraged a leak of the Cuban brigade story in order to undercut and kill SALT II ratification. Nicholas Thompson, *The Hawk and the Dove: Paul Nitze, George Kennan, and the History of the Cold War* (New York: Henry Holt, 2009), pp. 273–75.

7. Valentin M. Falin, *Bez skidok na obstoyatel'stvo: Politicheskiye vospominaniya* (Without allowance for circumstances: Political memoirs) (Moscow: Izd. Respublika, Izd. Sovremennik, 1999), pp. 361–62.

8. "Answer by L. I. Brezhnev to Questions by a Correspondent of 'Pravda,'" *Pravda*, January 13, 1980.

9. Garthoff, *Détente and Confrontation*, pp. 818–19.

10. The GRU estimate was ten to twelve minutes. The distance from possible Pershing II sites in West Germany to Moscow-area targets was greater than the range announced by the United States but within the range estimated and believed by Soviet military technical experts, based on their reading of US tests of the missile as well as assumptions as to US targeting priorities. The NATO decision was justified as a counter to Soviet deployment of modern intermediate-range missiles, called in the West SS-20, to replace obsolescent SS-4 and SS-5 missiles. The Soviet deployment was, as usual, not announced nor was the fact that it was a missile replacement, and an alarm was raised in Western Europe over what was seen as a threatening Soviet buildup. The United States did not see a military requirement for new NATO missiles, but it wanted to reassure its allies. Each side regarded its own missile deployment as keeping up the strategic balance through modernization but saw the deployment by the other side as ratcheting up the military confrontation. For further analysis of the episode, see ibid., pp. 935–74.

11. See ibid., pp. 991–1046, esp. pp. 1014–17, and Kryuchkov, *Lichnoye delo*, vol. 1, pp. 203–5.

12. Leonov, *Likholet'ye*, pp. 201–2; Kornienko, *Kholodnaya voina*, pp. 193–97; Garthoff, *Détente and Confrontation*, p. 1010.

13. Kryuchkov, *Lichnoye delo*, vol. 1, pp. 199–201 and 205.

14. Once the intervention occurred, the KGB's analysts erroneously predicted that the strong negative American reaction would be brief (Andrew and Gordievsky, *KGB*, p. 578). The KGB had made a similar estimate as to the Western reaction to Soviet military intervention in Czechoslovakia in 1968, which had proven correct.

15. See Raymond L. Garthoff, *The Great Transition: American-Soviet Relations and the End of the Cold War* (Washington: Brookings Institution, 1994), p. 59.

16. See Ben B. Fischer, *A Cold War Conundrum: The 1983 Soviet War Scare*, *CSI 92-10002* (Washington: Central Intelligence Agency, Center for the Study of Intelligence, September 1997), pp. 6–10, and Gregory L. Vistica, *Fall from Glory: The Men Who Sank the U.S. Navy* (New York: Simon & Schuster, 1995), pp. 8, 105–9, 116–32. The Soviets were shocked because the radio silence negated their advantage from having US Navy codes supplied by their agent John Walker (arrested in 1985). The commander, Adm. James "Ace" Lyons Jr., used the silent approach because he suspected Soviet intelligence was intercepting US naval communications. On these developments and Soviet reactions to the new administration, see Garthoff, *The Great Transition*, pp. 54–84. On the provocative American military demonstrations, see also David Hoffman, *The Dead Hand: The Untold Story of the Cold War Arms Race and Its Dangerous Legacy* (New York: Doubleday, 2009), pp. 63–71.

17. This Politburo meeting may have been the first attended by its newest member, Mikhail Gorbachev, raised from candidate to full voting membership in March 1981.

18. The most authoritative account, based on information from former KGB colonel Oleg Gordievsky, is in Andrew and Gordievsky, *Comrade Kryuchkov's Instructions*, pp. 67–69; also see Andrew and Gordievsky, *Sword and the Shield*, pp. 433–34.

19. Andrew and Gordievsky, *Comrade Kryuchkov's Instructions*, pp. 69–85. The KGB's instructions exaggerated the danger by citing an unrealistically short transit time of four to six minutes. As noted earlier, the GRU General Staff estimate was a more accurate ten to twelve minutes.

20. Ibid., p. 85.

21. See Vadim V. Bakatin, *Izbavleniye ot KGB* (Getting rid of the KGB) (Moscow: Novosti, 1992), pp. 89–90; A. Ivan'ko, "The End of VRYaN," *Izvestiya*, November 28, 1991, p. 1. In transition at the time, the new independent foreign intelligence service headed by Primakov was called the Central Intelligence Service (TSR), but within a month it officially became the SVR.

22. See Yuri B. Shvets, *Washington Station: My Life as a KGB Spy in America* (New York: Simon & Schuster, 1994), pp. 124–25. This document, if genuine, has not been declassified and cannot be confirmed. It was not, however, suppressed owing to doubts in Moscow about its validity but owing to its incompatibility with Soviet core beliefs.

23. Information from a knowledgeable former GRU officer.

24. Andrew and Gordievsky, *Comrade Kryuchkov's Instructions*, pp. 100–15; see esp. pp. 113–14.

25. Shvets, *Washington Station*, pp. 73–74.

26. Lt. Gen. V. F. Grushko, *Sud'ba razvedchika: kniga vospominanii* (The fate of an intelligence officer: A memoir) (Moscow: Mezhdunarodniye Otnosheniya, 1997), p. 132.

27. See Garthoff, *Great Transition*, p. 516, on the deception component of SDI testing and pp. 514–17 on Soviet reaction to SDI.

28. See ibid., pp. 118–31; Seymour Hersh, *"The Target Is Destroyed": What Really Happened to Flight 007 and What America Knew about It* (New York: Random House, 1986); Alexander Dallin, *Black Box: KAL 007 and the Superpowers* (Berkeley: University of California Press, 1985); and Marilyn J. Young and Michael K. Launer, *Flights of Fancy, Flight of Doom: KAL 007 and Soviet-American Rhetoric* (New York: University Press of America, 1988). The United States had recently been flying both "psywar" and reconnaissance flights in the same region, including overflying Soviet territory in one instance. See Fischer, *Cold War Conundrum*, pp. 9–10, and Hoffman, *Dead Hand*, pp. 63–71.

29. "Statement by General Secretary of the CC of the CPSU, Chairman of the Presidium of the Supreme Soviet of the USSR Yu. V. Andropov," *Pravda*, September 29, 1983.

30. This incident has been most fully researched by David Hoffman, who held three informative interviews with Petrov; see Hoffman, *Dead Hand*, pp. 6–11. Col. Gen. Yury V. Votintsev, "The Unknown Military Forces of a Vanishing Superpower," *Voenno-istoricheskii zhurnal* (The military-historical journal), no. 10 (October 1993): p. 38, first disclosed the event but apparently in error of memory referred to it as occurring in July. Petrov, incidentally, was upbraided for his action.

31. Andrew and Gordievsky, *Comrade Kryuchkov's Instructions*, pp. 85 and 87–88. See also Garthoff, *Great Transition*, pp. 138–40; Fischer, *Cold War Conundrum*, pp. 24–26; Fritz W. Ermarth, *Observations on the 'War Scare' of 1983 from an Intelligence Perch*, Parallel History Project on NATO and the Warsaw Pact, November 6, 2003; Stephen J. Cimbala, "Year of Maximum Danger? The 1983 'War Scare' and US-Soviet

Deterrence," *Journal of Slavic Military History Studies* 13, no. 2 (June 2000): pp. 1–24; Len Scott, "Intelligence and the Risk of Nuclear War: Able Archer-83 Revisited," *Intelligence and National Security* 26, no. 6 (December 2011), pp. 778–90; and Don Oberdorfer, *From the Cold War to a New Era: The United States and the Soviet Union, 1983–1991* (Baltimore: Johns Hopkins University Press, 1998), pp. 65–67.

32. Scott, "Intelligence and the Risk," p. 15.

33. Andrew and Mitrokhin, *World Was Going Our Way*, p. 414, on the Politburo statement; General Kalugin, *First Directorate*, p. 302, reports the KGB cable.

34. Andrew and Gordievsky, *Comrade Kryuchkov's Instructions*, pp. 4–6 and 17, from a January 1984 meeting and a November 2, 1983, instruction. For discussion of other statements of alarm by political and military leaders, see Garthoff, *Great Transition*, pp. 136–38.

35. See Kalugin, *First Directorate*, pp. 256–60.

36. This cooperative arrangement was first disclosed by Milt Bearden and James Risen, *The Main Enemy: The Inside Story of the CIA's Final Showdown with the KGB* (New York: Random House, 2003), pp. 189–90.

37. See Garthoff, *Great Transition*, pp. 142–94 for analysis of US-Soviet relations in 1984, on which this discussion draws.

38. Ibid., pp. 102–8 and 142–68, for the initial transition in Reagan's view of the possibility of a different relationship with the Soviet Union.

39. See detailed KGB instructions brought out by Colonel Gordievsky in 1985: Andrew and Gordievsky, *Comrade Kryuchkov's Instructions*, pp. 1–22 and 67–90, and Andrew and Gordievsky, *More Instructions*, pp. 1–24.

40. See Garthoff, *Great Transition*, pp. 159–60.

Chapter 5. Gorbachev

1. Garthoff, *Great Transition*, pp. 197–234.

2. A routine, if still provocative, US Navy foray into the Black Sea coastal area of Crimea in March 1986 intended to exercise a dubious interpretation of "innocent passage," over Soviet protests, had an unanticipated political effect. Unknown to those who authorized the action, Gorbachev was resting at a Soviet leadership dacha nearby at the time, and some in Moscow interpreted the action as a deliberate slap at Gorbachev for holding out in negotiations on the terms of another summit meeting that raised questions as to whether Gorbachev had been too trusting of Reagan. See ibid., pp. 269–70 and 273–74. I was told this

in confidence at the time by a senior Soviet official and also by Col. Gen. Nikolai Chervov of the General Staff and later in an interview by Gorbachev himself. The Soviet government protested the incursion, but Gorbachev's presence nearby was not mentioned, as that would only have drawn attention to Soviet impotence.

3. Anatoly Chernyayev, *Shest' let s Gorbachevym: Po dnevnikovym zapiskam* (Six years with Gorbachev: According to a diary record) (Moscow: Kultura, 1993), pp. 114–15. See also Dobrynin, *In Confidence*, p. 610.

4. For more full discussion and citations from Gorbachev's speech to the Twenty-Seventh Congress, see Garthoff, *Great Transition*, pp. 254–64.

5. See ibid., pp. 261–64, and on the 1970s, Garthoff, *Détente and Confrontation*, pp. 40–57. For the best analysis of the development of the new thinking, see Robert D. English, *Russia and the Idea of the West: Gorbachev, Intellectuals, and the End of the Cold War* (New York: Columbia University Press, 2000). On the role of transnational contacts, see Matthew Evangelista, *Unarmed Forces: The Transnational Movement to End the Cold War* (Ithaca, NY: Cornell University Press, 1999).

6. Akhromeyev and Kornienko, *Glazami marshala i diplomata*, pp. 69–73, 86–90, and 120–27; Hoffman, *Dead Hand*, pp. 235–37, 270–72, and 275; and see Raymond L. Garthoff, *Deterrence and the Revolution in Soviet Military Doctrine* (Washington: Brookings Institution, 1990), pp. 94–185.

7. Marshal Akhromeyev, in ibid., pp. 69 and 70.

8. Ibid., pp. 123 and 125. See also Hoffman, *Dead Hand*, pp. 270–72 and 275.

9. Akhromeyev and Kornienko, *Glazami marshala i diplomata*, p. 122. Emphasis added.

10. Ibid., p. 126. It should also be noted that in 1990–91 a number of the military leaders who had contributed to the revision of strategy and doctrine in 1986 and its implementation in 1986–89, including notably its prime mover, Marshal Akhromeyev, became disenchanted, not with their revised doctrine and actions implementing it in the late 1980s but in what they saw as American propensity to take advantage of the Soviet Union in negotiations on arms limitations (and the terms of German reunification in particular), and even more so in the acceptance of this inequality by Gorbachev and Shevardnadze, who rarely consulted the military. They too wanted to wind down the Cold War but as equal partners with the United States and the Western Europeans, with due regard to Soviet security interests, and not as subservient petitioners.

11. Chernyayev, *Shest' let s Gorbachevym*, p. 114, and see p. 144.

12. "From the Gorbachev Archives," *Mirovaya ekonomika i mezhdunarodnyye otnosheniya* (The world economy and international relations), no. 11 (November 1993): p. 75.

13. E. Shevardnadze, in *Vestnik Ministerstva Inostrannykh del SSSR* (Bulletin of the Ministry of Foreign Affairs of the USSR), no. 15 (August 15, 1988): pp. 32 and 40; Anatoly Kovalev, ibid., p. 37; and Vladimir Petrovsky, ibid., p. 55.

14. Kovalev, ibid., p. 37.

15. Kryuchkov, *Lichnoye delo*, vol. 1, p. 333.

16. For example, see Grushko, *Sud'ba razvedchika*, p. 190.

17. Ibid., p. 201. General Shebarshin also has noted that while relations between Gorbachev and Kryuchkov were initially good, they faded, and after 1989 Kryuchkov became more critical of Gorbachev (*Iz zhizni*, pp. 22 and 35–36).

18. Shvets, *Washington Station*, p. 237.

19. For a translation of Kryuchkov's speech from *Mezhdunarodnaya zhizn'*, no. 10 (October 1988), see Andrew and Gordievsky, *Comrade Kryuchkov's Instructions*, see pp. 213–17. Emphasis added. Kryuchkov also cited concern over SDI, which he told me in 1999 had in his view been a disinformation bluff from the outset.

20. The annual reports of the KGB to Gorbachev covering the years 1985, 1986, 1988, and 1989 are available, and the one for 1986 (submitted in February 1987) was the last to refer briefly to "acquiring information in the interests of timely warning of a surprise nuclear-missile attack on the USSR." The issues reviewing 1988 and 1989 make no reference to the program. See Raymond L. Garthoff, "The KGB Reports to Gorbachev," *Intelligence and National Security* 11, no. 2 (April 1996): p. 228.

21. See Richard Popplewell, "Themes in the Rhetoric of KGB Chairmen from Andropov to Kryuchkov," *Intelligence and National Security* 6, no. 3 (1991): pp. 513–47.

22. Garthoff, "KGB Reports to Gorbachev," p. 230. Emphasis added.

23. Bakatin, *Izbavleniye ot KGB*, p. 176.

24. For a detailed account, see Garthoff, *Great Transition*, pp. 220–26 and 268–85.

25. For reference to the document and KGB chairman Viktor Chebrikov's report of a meeting of KGB leaders on December 10 where they pledged to correct their ways, see Garthoff, "KGB Reports to Gorbachev," pp. 226–27 and 242.

26. See Shvets, *Washington Station*, p. 236.

27. Chernyayev, *Shest' let s Gorbachevym*, p. 285.

28. Leonov, *Likholet'ye*, p. 121. For an evaluation of KGB (and CIA) threat assessments of the adversary in 1975–91, in particular on changes under Gorbachev, see Mikhail A. Alexeev, *Without Warning: Threat Assessment, Intelligence, and Global Struggle* (New York: St. Martin's, 1997), pp. 181–225. For evaluations of Soviet intelligence assessment by two experienced British intelligence assessors, see Percy Cradock, *Know Your Enemy: How the Joint Intelligence Committee Saw the World* (London: John Murray, 2002), pp. 281–89, and Gordon S. Barrass, *The Great Cold War: A Journey through the Hall of Mirrors* (Stanford, CA: Stanford University Press, 2009), pp. 379–400. For an unconvincing account seeking to demonstrate a threatening Soviet "war scare" since the early 1980s, see Peter Vincent Pry, *War Scares: Russia and America on the Nuclear Brink* (Westport, CT: Praeger, 1999).

29. Chernyayev, *Shest' let s Gorbachevym*, pp. 281, 288, and 301.

30. Ibid., pp. 301–4; and see Dobrynin, *In Confidence*, pp. 632–34.

31. Lt. Gen. L. Shebarshin, interview by John Kampfner, *Daily Telegraph* (London), December 1, 1992.

32. Leonov, *Likholet'ye*, p. 333, and see p. 317.

33. Ibid., p. 317.

34. Garthoff, "KGB Reports to Gorbachev," pp. 224, 227.

35. Shebarshin, *Iz zhizni*, pp. 92–93.

36. Mikhail Gorbachev, *Zhizn' i reformy* (Life and reforms), vol. 2 (Moscow: Novosti, 1995), p. 36.

37. See Garthoff, *Great Transition*, p. 435, for this episode, disclosed by Gorbachev's Foreign Ministry interpreter. General Kryuchkov told me, in a private conversation in Moscow in 1999, that he believed the United States had intentionally provoked Saddam Hussein into occupying Kuwait in order to have an excuse for attacking him; getting Soviet support was just frosting on the cake.

38. Grushko has revealed that the KGB reporting to Gorbachev involved the Western disinformation claim. See Grushko, *Sud'ba razvedchika*, pp. 201–2. In 1999 Kryuchkov recounted to me the same incident—but omitted mentioning that the KGB added the claim of Western disinformation

39. Leonov, *Likholet'ye*, pp. 320–22.

40. See Akhromeyev and Kornienko, *Glazami marshala i diplomata*, pp. 86–90, and Dobrynin, *In Confidence*, pp. 596–98.

41. For an analysis at the time noting these broader purposes and possibilities, see Raymond L. Garthoff, "The Gorbachev Proposal and Prospects

for Arms Control," *Arms Control Today* 16 (January/February 1986): pp. 3–6.

42. E. Shevardnadze, in *Vestnik Ministerstva Inostrannykh del SSSR* (Bulletin of the Ministry of Foreign Affairs of the USSR), no. 15 (August 15, 1988): pp. 32 and 40; Anatoly Kovalev, ibid., p. 37; Andrew and Gordievsky, *Comrade Kryuchkov's Instructions*, pp. 213–14, for a translation of Kryuchkov's speech from *Mezhdunarodnaya zhizn'*, no. 10 (October 1988).

43. Kirpichenko, *Razvedka*, p. 340.

44. Shebarshin, *Iz zhizni*, pp. 221–23 and 257–59. General Grushko also stated that by 1990 the United States was no longer the main adversary but a partner. Grushko, *Sud'ba razvedchika*, p. 171.

45. For all the declarations, see Garthoff, *Great Transition*, pp. 406, 432, and 434.

46. Galina Sidorova, "A Non-Christmas Story," *New Times*, no. 52 (December 25–31, 1990).

47. I had heard about this, and when I asked Baklanov about it in 1999, he proudly confirmed it.

48. In addition to former Soviet intelligence officers' later memoirs, there is much evidence of their warnings in 1989–91. See Andrew and Gordievsky, *KGB*, pp. 606–8 and 623–28.

49. Kryuchkov, *Lichnoye delo*, vol. 1, pp. 353–60.

50. Grushko, *Sud'ba razvedchika*, pp. 175, 195, 196, and 201.

51. Leonov, *Likholet'ye*, pp. 372 and 375–76. Emphasis added.

52. Kryuchkov, a leading figure among the conservatives involved in the soft coup, also was a leader of the more drastic pseudo coup in August, but he did not bring the KGB as an organization into his political activities. He did not involve other KGB leaders in the August attempt (which sought to coerce Gorbachev into abandoning the effort to negotiate a new union of constituent republics to replace the USSR) except for directing Lt. Gen. Yury Plekhanov, the head of the security directorate, to isolate Gorbachev. He and his coconspirators had no "Plan B" when the plot failed.

53. Kryuchkov, *Lichnoye delo*, vol. 1, pp. 414–20, citing his speech of June 17, 1991 (and for an abridged text, see vol. 2, pp. 387–92). Several KGB generals in their memoirs have referred to Gorbachev, Aleksandr Yakovlev, and Shevardnadze as "objectively" giving up (if not selling out) Soviet interests to the Americans, but Kryuchkov has gone further in claiming that Yakovlev was a US "agent of influence," recruited while

an exchange graduate student at Columbia University in 1968. He even argued this with Gorbachev in 1990, to no avail. He repeated this claim in a meeting at which I was present in June 1999.

54. See the aforecited *Ocherki istorii Rossiskoi razvedki*, vol. 6 (2005), pp. 20–38. *Schweizer's Victory: The Reagan Administration's Secret Strategy That Hastened the Collapse of the Soviet Union* (New York: Atlantic Monthly Press, 1994) was published in 1995 in Russian translation (although not in Russia but in Belarus).

55. See Kryuchkov, *Lichnoye delo*, vol. 1, p. 420. He made the same statement in a speech in December 1990 (cited in Andrew and Gordievsky, *Comrade Kryuchkov's Instructions*, p. 218). See also Shebarshin, *Iz zhizni*, p. 180; Bobkov, *KGB i vlast'*, p. 369; Grushko, *Sud'ba razvedchika*, p. 195; and Kirpichenko, *Razvedka*, p. 33.

56. Kirpichenko, *Razvedka*, p. 33.

Conclusions

1. Georgy Arbatov, *Zatyanuvsheyesya vyzdorovleniye (1953–1985 gg.): Svidetel'stvo sovremennika* (A long drawn-out convalescence, 1953–1985: A contemporary witness) (Moscow: Mezhdunarodniye Otnosheniya, 1991), p. 267.

2. And years later, the official *Essays on the History of Russian Foreign Intelligence* stated with reference to the Cold War that "yadernoye ustrasheniye" (nuclear deterrence by intimidation) after 1945 became "the main political and military strategy of the United States." See *Ocherki istorii Rossiiskoi vneshnei razvedki*, vol. 5 (2003), pp. 36–37.

3. Col. Gen. N. F. Chervov, "On the Path to Trust and Security," *Voennaya mysl'* (Military thought), no. 6 (June 1990): p. 14.

4. Lt. Gen. V. Kirpichenko, in an interview in "Foreign Intelligence: From the USSR to Russia," *Krasnaya zvezda* (Red star), October 30, 1993, p. 6. General Kirpichenko was at that time a senior consultant to the SVR, the Russian Foreign Intelligence Service.

5. See *Osnovnyye polozheniya voyennoi doktriny Rossiiskoi Federatsii* (Main provisions of the military doctrine of the Russian Federation), *Voyennaya mysl'* (Military thought), special issue (November 1993): p. 4. Even earlier, evolving Soviet military doctrine from 1987 to 1991 did not specify that the United States or NATO was "the enemy."

Index

Abakumov, Viktor, 104
"Able Archer," 67–70
Academy of Sciences (Soviet Union), 39, 41, 78
Academy of Social Sciences (Soviet Union), 77
Acheson, Dean, 69
"active measures," 47–48, 84
Adzhubei, Aleksei, 33
Afghanistan: Soviet Invasion of, xviii, 57, 59–60, 123n1, 123n5, 125n14; US policy and, 94
Akhromeyev, Sergei, 46, 68, 79, 80, 128n10
Albania, 8
Algeria, 26
Andreotti, Giulio, 86
Andropov, Yury, 39, 50, 52, 63, 83, 96, 99, 104; Afghanistan and, 59–60; appointment of, 40–41; biases of, 41–42, 48; death of, 71; propaganda and, 45; Reagan and, 66–68; "Theses of a Soviet Intelligence Doctrine for the 1970s" (Andropov), 44–45; VRYaN and, 61–63, 68–69
"Anti-Party Group," 17, 22
Arbatov, Georgy, 39–40, 59, 78, 82, 97
Ardahan, 2–3
Austria, 2

Bakatin, Vadim, 63, 84, 104
Baklanov, Oleg, 91, 131n47
Baltic states, 8
Baruch Plan, xiv
Bay of Pigs invasion by Cuban exiles in 1961, 26, 33
Bear Island, 2

Bentley, Elizabeth, 113n35
Beria, Lavrenty, 15, 16, 104, 114n41
Berlin, 6. *See also* East Berlin; West Berlin
Berlin Blockade, xvii, 11–12
Berlin Crisis, 23–24, 27, 28–29, 29–31, 42
Berlin Wall, xviii, 24
Blunt, Anthony, 108n5
Bogomolov, Oleg, 78
Bohlen, Charles, 21
Bol'shakov, Georgy, 27, 30, 117n21
Bornholm Island, 2
Brezhnev, Leonid: Afghanistan and, 59–60; ascension of, x, 37; détente and, 38–39, 52–54, 59; intelligence improvements under, 40–41; Khrushchev vs., 38; military buildups and, 37–38; at Moscow summit, 55; nuclear age and, 96; problems with intelligence given to, 46, 49; US-China alliance and, 43; at Vienna summit, 58
"Brezhnev Doctrine," 60
Brzezinski, Zbigniew, 53, 123n3
Bulganin, Nikolai, 20
Bulgaria, 2, 3, 23
Burgess, Guy, 6, 108n5
Bush, George H.W.: at Chernenko's funeral, 74; Gorbachev and, 74, 91; on KAL Flight 007, 69; at Malta, xviii, 86, 91, 100; on Soviet hegemony, 69–70
Byrnes, James, 10

Cairncross, John, 108n5
"Cambridge Five," 4–5, 6, 108n5, 108n7

Canada, 41, 51, 107n3, 113n35
Carlucci, Frank, 115n7
Carter, Jimmy: Brezhnev and, 53;
    Chinese relations and, 123n3;
    criticism of Soviet leaders by,
    124n5; at Vienna summit, 58
Casey, William, 64
"Center," 5. See KGB
Central Intelligence Agency (CIA).
    See CIA (Central Intelligence
    Agency)
Central Intelligence Service (TSR),
    125n21
"Chance for Peace" (Eisenhower), 18
"Charioteer," 110n16
Chebrikov, Viktor, 83–84, 104,
    129n25
"Checkpoint Charlie," Berlin
    confrontation in 1961, 29–31
Chernenko, Konstantin, 71, 74
Chernyayev, Anatoly, 75, 78
Chervov, Nikolai, 98–99, 127n2,
    128n2
China: Brezhnev and, 37; communist
    victory in, xiii, 11; Khrushchev
    and, 23; Soviet force buildup
    and, 37; Soviet relationship with,
    deterioration of, 42–44, 119n37;
    Soviet withdrawal from, 2;
    strengthening of, xiii; US relations
    with, improvement of, 42–43, 58,
    123n3; US visits to, 43; Vietnam
    War and, 44
Churchill, Winston: "Iron Curtain"
    speech of, xvii, 8, 64, 111n21; and
    proposal for a "summit" meeting
    in 1953, 17; Roosevelt and, 4; Stalin
    and, 4
CIA (Central Intelligence Agency):
    Andropov and, 69; Czechoslovakia
    and, 45; Gorbachev and, 86, 88, 93;
    KGB hotline with, 70; KGB vs.,
    in staffing, 41; Khrushchev and,

25, 28; Soviet view of, 47; Stalin's
    delusion about Molotov and CIA,
    16
Clay, Lucius, 30
codebreaking, 114n35
Cold War, xi–xv
Cominform, 11
Comintern, 113n31
Commissariat for Internal Affairs
    (NKVD), 12, 15, 113n31
Committee for State Security (KGB).
    See KGB
Committee on Information (KI), 13,
    14–15, 21, 113n34. See also "Small
    KI"
Committee on the Present Danger,
    69, 72
Communist International
    (Comintern), 113n31
Communist Party of the Soviet
    Union (CPSU), 32–33
Communist Party USA (CPUSA),
    41, 48
Council for Security and
    Cooperation in Europe (CSCE),
    53, 55, 57
counterintelligence, 8, 15, 47–48, 65
CPSU (Communist Party of the
    Soviet Union), 32–33
CPUSA (Communist Party USA), 41
Crimea, 127n2
CSCE (Council for Security and
    Cooperation in Europe), 53, 55, 57
Cuba, 33; Soviet "combat brigade"
    crisis, 58, 124n6
Cuban Missile Crisis, xviii, 26–27,
    33–35, 42, 63, 68
Czechoslovakia, 2, 11, 45, 51, 125n14

Dardanelles Straits, 3
defection of Soviet intelligence
    operatives, 48, 113n35
Defense Council, 37, 79–80

Defense Industry Department, 37
de Gaulle, Charles, 50
Dekanozov, Vladimir, 3
Democratic Republic of Congo, 26
Denmark, 2
détente, 37–42, 44–45, 49–55, 58–59, 60–61, 71, 76–77
deterrence, 97–98; Brezhnev and, 37; credible, 70; Khrushchev and, 17, 20, 35; Mikoyan and, 18; missile defense and, 64; mutual, 35, 37, 78; "new thinking" and, 81, 82; Reagan and, 70; in Russian, 98, 132n2; superoffensive capabilities and, 97–98
Dillon, Douglas, 26
disinformation, 28, 43, 47–48, 65–66, 89, 129n19
Dobrynin, Anatoly, 43, 49, 56, 122n32
Donovan, "Wild Bill," 108n9
Dornan, Robert, 65
"Dropshot," 6–7, 109n13, 109n14
Drozdov, Yury, 109n14
Dulles, Allen, 25, 26
Dulles, John Foster, 18, 115n2, 116n14

East Berlin, 29–30
East Germany, 3, 11, 21, 23, 28, 29–30, 114n41
Eastern Europe, 21, 76, 79
Egypt, 21–22
Eisenhower, Dwight: Khrushchev and, 17–18, 25, 28; "Open Skies" proposal of, 21, 116n10; U-2 shootdown and, 25; Zhukov and, 21
Ethiopia, 3
European security, 51

Falin, Valentin, 14, 59
Federal Republic of Germany. See West Germany
Fedorchuk, Vitaly, 104
Fedotov, Pyotr, 105

Feklisov, Aleksandr, 7
Finland, 2, 11
First Chief Directorate (PGU), 13–14, 40–41, 45–47, 59–60, 62, 105
Fitin, Pavel, 4, 105, 108n7
Ford, Gerald: Brezhnev and, 57; détente and, 54; Helsinki Accords and, 53
Foreign Intelligence Service (SVR), 63, 99, 105
Foreign Ministry (Soviet Union), 16, 40, 49, 77, 99
Foreign Office (United Kingdom), Soviet penetration of, 4–5
Foreign Policy Department (OVP), 113n31
Four Power summit, 25
France: détente and, 50; Four Power summit in, 25; Soviet intelligence penetration in, 15; in Suez Crisis, 21–22

"Gavrilov channel," a KGB-CIA direct communication connection, 70
General Department (of the Central Committee), 48, 71
General Staff, 79–81
Geneva summit, 20–21, 64, 74–75
German Democratic Republic. See East Germany
German reunification, 93
Germany, after World War II, xii, 2, 3. See also East Germany; West Germany
Gilpatric, Roswell, 29
"Global Shield," 63
Gorbachev, Mikhail: on Able Archer, 68; arms reduction and, 128n10; ascension of, xi, xviii, 74; Bush, George H.W. and, 74, 91; in coup, 131n52; and Crimean foray of US Navy, 127n2; détente and,

Gorbachev, Mikhail (*continued*)
76–77; at Geneva, 75; Gulf War
and, 88–89; on intelligence, 88;
intelligence reporting and, 85–86,
87–88; KGB and, 85–86, 87–88,
90–91; Kryuchkov on, 131n53; at
Malta, xviii, 86, 91; "new thinking"
and, 76–77, 81–82, 87; "peaceful
coexistence" and, 115n7; Reagan
and, 74–75, 100; at Reykjavik,
xviii, 75; significance of, 100;
Soviet downfall and, 92–93; Star
Wars program and, 65, 89–90
Gordievsky, Oleg, 41, 70
Great Britain. *See* United Kingdom
Grechko, Andrei, 37, 50, 52
Greece, 8, 11
Grenada, 64
Gromyko, Andrei: Afghanistan and,
59–60; China and, 43; Cuban
Missile Crisis and, 34; détente and,
49–50, 59, 74–75; Foreign Ministry
role and, 16; intelligence and, 16;
on Kennedy, 26; on his objectivity,
114n40; in Politburo, 52; as titular
president, 75
"Group North," 47
GRU (Main Intelligence Directorate
of the General Staff), 13, 27, 28,
46–47, 49, 59, 81, 124n10
Grushko, Viktor, 65, 89, 92, 130n38,
131n44
Gulf War, 88–89, 130n37
Guzenko, Igor, 113n35

Harriman, Averell, 3–4, 36
Helsinki Accord, 53, 57, 123n38
Helsinki Conference, 51, 53, 55, 106
Hiroshima, xiv–xv
Hokkaido, 2
hotline: direct crisis connection
between US and USSR, 36, 54
Hottelet, Richard, 4

Hungary, 2, 3, 21, 33
Hussein, Saddam, 88–89, 130n37

ideology, 96–98; in 1980s, 77; China
and, 44; détente and, 39; Gorbachev
and, 75; of Marxism-Leninism, xi–
xii, 17; Reagan and, 75
Ignatyev, Semyon, 104
IMEMO (Institute of the World
Economy and International
Relations), 39, 41
Information-Analytical Department,
40
Information Directorate, 113n31
Information Service (SI) of the Central
Committee, 14, 113n31, 116n14
Inozemtsev, Nikolai, 41, 78
Institute of the USA (Soviet Union),
39–40
Institute of the World Economy and
International Relations (IMEMO),
39, 41
intelligence assessment: under
Brezhnev, 39–49; under Gorbachev,
85–93, 130n28; under Khrushchev,
28–32; under Stalin, 12–16
intelligence services: under Brezhnev,
40–41; in Cuban Missile Crisis,
34; improvement of Soviet, 13–15;
Soviet penetration of British, 4–5,
108n5; under Stalin, 4–8, 10, 12–16;
as threat, in view of opposing
intelligence services, 97–98. *See
also* CIA (Central Intelligence
Agency); GRU (Main Intelligence
Directorate); KGB (Committee for
State Security); KI (Committee on
Information)
"intelligence war:" US vs. USSR,
47–50, 84
International Department (of the
Central Committee), 48–49,
77–78, 87

International Information
Department (OMI), 13, 59, 113n31
Iran, 3, 14–15, 60
Iraq, 22, 23, 88–89, 130n37
"Iron Curtain" speech (Churchill),
xvii, 8, 64, 111n21
Italy, 2
Ivanov, Semyon, 32

Japan: Soviet exclusion from
occupation of, 2; US nuclear
bombing of, xiv–xv
Jervis, Robert, x
Johnson, Lyndon, 36, 38–39
Joint Chiefs of Staff (JCS), 6
Jordan, 22–23

Kaganovich, Lazar, 52
KAL (Korean Air Lines) Flight 007,
xviii, 66–67, 68, 69, 126n28
Kalugin, Oleg, 45, 49, 68–69
Karpov, Viktor, 14
Karpovich, Georgy, 27
Kars, 2–3
Kennan, George, 8–9, 13, 111n22
Kennedy, John F.: in Berlin Crisis,
30; in Cuban Missile Crisis, xviii,
26–27, 34–35; KGB analysis of, 26;
Khrushchev and, 26–27, 28–29,
33–36
KGB (Committee for State Security):
Afghanistan and, 59–60, 125n14;
Andropov and, 44–45; Annual
Reports (1960, 117n16; 1967,
121n17; 1985, 1986, 1988, 1989,
129n20); under Brezhnev, 41;
Chinese-Soviet relationship and,
43; CIA hotline with, 70; in coup,
91–92, 131n52; disinformation
by, problems with, 47–49;
distortion of information from,
45; Gorbachev and, 85–86,
87–88, 90–91; Gulf War and, 89;
heads, 104; ignoring of, by Soviet
officials, 45–46; on Kennedy, 26;
Khrushchev's US views and, 25;
national liberation movements
and, 57; "new thinking" and, 83–
84; in nuclear missile intelligence,
59; political reporting of, as
lacking, 41; recruitment at, 41; role
in the abortive August 1991 coup,
131n52; Soviet downfall and, 91–93;
Star Wars program and, 64–65,
89–90; US war plans and, 62–63,
125n19, 129n20; waning influence
of, 87–88, 89–90
Khrushchev, Nikita: ascension of,
17; in Berlin Crisis, 23–24, 28–29,
30–31; Brezhnev vs., 38; in China,
42; in Cuban Missile Crisis, 26–27,
33–35, 42; Eisenhower and, 17–18,
25; at Geneva summit, 20–21;
intelligence skepticism of, 28;
Kennedy and, 26–27, 28–29, 35–
36; lessons learned, x; nuclear age
and, 96; opposing Malenkov, 17–
20, 115n4; ouster of, 36; "peaceful
coexistence" doctrine and, 20; in
Suez Crisis, 21–211; U-2 shootdown
and, 25; US visit by, 24–25
Khrushchev, Sergei, 22
KI (Committee on Information),
13–15, 21, 113n34, 115n2. See also
"Small KI"
Kirpichenko, Vadim, 12, 46, 47, 49,
90, 94, 99
Kissinger, Henry, 43, 51, 53, 58–59,
123n36
Korean Air Lines (KAL) Flight 007,
xviii, 66, 68, 69
Korean War, xvii, 11, 12
Kornienko, Georgy, 14, 59, 68,
116n14, 122n33
Kosygin, Aleksei, 122n35
Kovalev, Anatoly, 82

Kozlov, Frol, 24
Kruglov, Sergei, 104, 115n41
Kryuchkov, Vladimir, 46–47, 68,
    82–93, 96, 104–5; Afghanistan and,
    59–60; appointment to head PGU,
    40–41; in coup, 131n52; on Gulf
    War, 130n37; on Helsinki Accord,
    123n38; relations with Gorbachev,
    129n17, 130n38; Star Wars (SDI)
    program and, 65, 129n19
Kubatkin, Pyotr, 105
Kurchatov, Igor, 115n4
Kuwait, 88–89, 130n37
Kuznetsov, Fyodor, 15

Lebanon, 22–23
Lee, Duncan, 108n9
Leonov, Nikolai, 40–42, 44–45, 59–
    60, 86, 87, 89, 92–93, 123n1, 123n38
Libya, 3
Litvinov, Maksim, 1, 3
"Live Oak," NATO military
    contingency plans passed to
    Moscow, 27
local wars, Soviet view of, 26, 119n2
"Long Telegram" (Kennan), 8–9, 13,
    111n23
Lyons, James, 125n16

Maclean, Donald, 4, 10, 108n5
Main Intelligence Directorate
    (GRU), 13, 27, 28, 46–47, 59, 81
Maisky, Ivan, 1
Malenkov, Georgy, 15, 17, 18–19,
    115n4
Malik, Yakov, 14
Malta Conference, xviii, 86, 91, 100
Malyshev, Vyacheslav, 115n4
Manchuria, 2
Marshall Plan, xvii, 10, 112n27
Marx, Karl, 20
Marxism-Leninism, xi–xii, 17
May, Ernest, x

MBFR (mutual and balanced force
    reductions), 51
Mendelyevich, Lev, 14
Merkulov, Vsevolod, 104
MGB (Ministry of State Security), 13,
    14, 104, 105, 113n31. See also KGB
    (Committee for State Security)
Middle East, 22–23
Mikoyan, Anastas, 16, 18, 24–25,
    115n4
military doctrine: post-Soviet, 99;
    Soviet, 79–81
military exercises, 32, 43, 61, 63,
    67–70, 79
military expansion, Soviet, 37–38
military intelligence, 46–47, 59
Military Thought (journal), 98
military warning systems, 67–70. See
    also VRYaN (Surprise Nuclear-
    Missile Attack)
Ministry of Defense (Soviet Union),
    40, 79–81
Ministry of Internal Affairs (MVD),
    104, 105, 114n41
Ministry of State Security (MGB), 13,
    14, 104, 105, 113n31. See also KGB
    (Committee for State Security)
missile defense, 64–66
missile gap, 24, 29
missiles, 22, 26–27, 59, 64, 124n10
Molotov, Vyacheslav, xiv, 1, 9, 11,
    52, 96, 115n4; Iran and, 14–15;
    Khrushchev and, 17; KI and, 13–14,
    16; Novikov and, 111n23, 112n27; in
    Stalin's paranoia, 16
Montgomery, Bernard, 6
Mortin, Fyodor, 105
Moscow summit (1972), 50, 51, 55
Moscow summit (1988), 115n7
Mossadeq, Mohammed, 14–15
mutual and balanced force reductions
    (MBFR), 51
mutual deterrence, 17, 33

MVD (Ministry of Internal Affairs), 104, 105, 114n41

national liberation wars and movements, 26, 57, 123n2
National Security Council Report 68 (NSC-68), 7, 109n15
NATO (North Atlantic Treaty Organization): détente and, 51; founding of, xvii, 11; KGB and, 62; missile deployment and, 59–60, 124n10; Soviet intelligence penetration of, 27, 31–32, 118n32; Syria and, 22; Warsaw Pact and, 51–52. *See also* "Able Archer," 67–70
"new thinking," 76–83, 86–87
Nitze, Paul, 124n6
Nixon, Richard: Brezhnev and, 53, 57, 123n36; in China in 1972, 43; détente and, 51, 54, 59; at Moscow summit, 50, 55; Soviet visit by, as vice president in 1959, 24
NKGB (People's Commissariat for State Security), 4, 104, 113n31
NKVD (Commissariat for Internal Affairs), 12, 15, 113n31
North Atlantic Treaty Organization (NATO). *See* NATO (North Atlantic Treaty Organization)
Norway, 2, 61
Novikov, Nikolai, 9–11, 111n23, 112n27
NSC-68, 7, 109n15
nuclear age, xiii–xv, 18, 95–96
nuclear arms race, 18
nuclear arms reduction, 18, 51, 61, 128n10
nuclear deterrence, 97–98
Nuclear-Missile Attack (RYaN), 62. *See also* Surprise Nuclear-Missile Attack (VRYaN)
nuclear missiles, 22, 24–27, 29, 59, 64, 124n10

nuclear test ban, 35–36, 119n42
nuclear war, 18–20, 28, 32–33, 62–63

Ochetto, Achille, 86
Office of Strategic Services (OSS), Soviet penetration of, 5, 108n9
OMI (International Information Department), 13, 59, 113n31
"On the Path to Trust and Security" (Chervov), 98
"Open Skies," 21, 116n10
Operation Unthinkable, 6
Ostpolitik, 51
OVP (Foreign Policy Department), 113n31

Panyushkin, Aleksandr S., 14, 105, 113n33
Paris CSCE summit meeting in 1990, 90
Paris Four Power summit meeting in 1960 aborted, 25
"peaceful coexistence," 17, 20, 33, 115n7
Penkovsky, Oleg, 32
People's Commissariat for State Security (NKGB), 104, 113n31
"people's democracies," xiii
perception, in international relations studies, x; in Soviet thinking, xi–xv; 96–97, 99
Pershing II missiles, 59, 62, 64, 124n10, 125n19
Petrov, Stanislav, 67, 126n30
PGU (*Pervoe glavnoe upravlenyie*), 13–14, 40–41, 45–47, 49, 59–60, 62, 85, 86, 105, 120n6
Philby, Kim, 4–5, 8, 108n5
Pitovranov, Yevgeny, 105
Plekhanov, Yury, 131n52
Podgorny, Nikolai, 52, 122n35
Poland, 3, 8, 21, 94
policy intelligence, 48

Politburo, 15, 17, 19, 29, 50, 52, 56, 61–62, 87, 99, 112n27, 129n17. *See also* Presidium

Ponomarev, Boris, 49, 77

Post-Hostilities Planning Committee, 5–6

Potsdam Conference, 2, 8, 20, 106

Presidium, 15, 19, 33. *See also* Politburo

Primakov, Yevgeny, 41, 63, 78, 105, 125n21

prisoners of war, 2

propaganda, 25, 39, 45, 47–48, 59

Pushkin, Georgy, 116n14

Putin, Vladimir, 101

Quemoy, 23, 116n14

Reagan, Ronald: Andropov's assessment of policy under, 66–67; bombing joke by, 72–73; Chernenko and, 74; decline in relations under, 57; détente and, 61; at Geneva, 75; Gorbachev and, 74–75, 100; improvement in relations under, 70–72; on Korean Airlines Flight 007, 66; military harassment of Soviet Union under, 61; "peaceful coexistence" and, 115n7; polemics of, 63–64; at Reykjavik, xviii, 75; second term of, 71–72; Star Wars program and, 64

"Reagan II," 71–72

"Red Orchestra," 5

Reykjavik, xviii, 75, 89, 100, 106

Richardson, Elliot, 43

Romania, 2, 3

Roosevelt, Franklin, xvii, 3, 4, 10, 36

Rusk, Dean, 27

Russia, 69, 99, 100–101

RYaN (Nuclear-Missile Attack), 62. *See also* VRYaN (Surprise Nuclear-Missile Attack)

Ryasnoy, Vasily, 105

Sagdeyev, Roald, 65

Sakharovsky, Aleksandr, 105

Savchenko, Sergei, 105

Schweizer, Peter, 94

SDI (Strategic Defense Initiative), 64–66, 89–90, 129n19

Secret Intelligence Service (MI-6; United Kingdom), Soviet penetration of, 4–5

Semichastny, Vladimir, 104

Serov, Ivan, 104

Shebarshin, Leonid, 47, 87, 88, 90, 105, 129n17

Shelepin, Aleksandr, 27, 52, 104

Shelest, Pyotr, 50, 52

Shevardnadze, Eduard, 74–75, 128n10, 131n53

Shlykov, Vitaly, 121n23

Shultz, George, 66, 70, 71, 74, 82, 88, 115n7

Shustov, Vladimir, 111n23

SI (Information Service), 113n31

"Small KI," 14–15, 113n34, 116n14

Snow, Edgar, 3

South Korea. *See* Korean Air Lines Flight 007; Korean War

Soviet Union: in Afghanistan, xviii, 57, 123n5, 125n14; after World War II, xii–xv, 1–3; Chinese relationship with, deterioration of, 42–44; collaboration by, in World War II, 1; coup in, xviii, 91–92, 93, 131n52; defensive shift in military policy in, 79–80; deterioration in relations with, 57–58; dissolution of, xviii, 91–93; improvement of relations with, 70–72; intelligence infiltration by, 4–6, 15–16, 27, 31–32, 108n5, 118n32; intelligence services improvement in, 13–15; Iran and, 3, 14–15; "Iron Curtain"

speech and, 8, 111n21; Korean
Air Lines Flight 007 shootdown
by, xviii, 66, 68, 69; Korean War
and, 11, 12; Marshall Plan and,
10; military expansion in, 37–38;
military intelligence in, 46–47, 59;
and national liberation movements
in Third World, 57, 123n2; nuclear
technology acquisition by, xiv,
4, 18; Reagan's bombing joke
and, 72–73; "security perimeter"
around, 1; Star Wars program
and, 64–66; trade war against, 94;
US confrontation of, 61–62; US
in view of, ix, 9, 55–56, 99; US
military exercises and, 67–70; US
plan for end of, 93–94; US war
plans for, 6–8, 62, 110n16, 125n19,
129n20; Vietnam War and, 44;
World War II intelligence of, 12.
See also Russia
Special Operations Executive, 5
Spitsbergen, 2
Sputnik, 22
SS-20 missiles, 124n10
Stalin, Josef: criticisms of, 3–4; death
of, xvii, 15, 16, 114n41; intelligence
and, 12, 15; Litvinov and, 3;
Litvinov on, 3–4; Marshall Plan
and, 10; Mossadeq and, 14–15;
nuclear age and, xiv; on nuclear
war, 7–8, 19; paranoia of, 16;
postwar order and, 1–2; Truman
and, 8; on United States, ix, 15–16;
view of Western leaders of, 4
"Star Wars," 64–66, 89–90. *See also*
SDI
stereotypes, 56
Strategic Defense Initiative (SDI),
64–66, 89–90
Sudoplatov, Pavel, 7–8
Suez Crisis, 21–22
Surprise Nuclear-Missile Attack

(VRYaN), 62–63, 67–69, 72, 79,
81, 83
Suslov, Mikhail, 49, 50, 52
SVR (Foreign Intelligence Service),
63, 99, 105, 117n24, 125n21, 132n4
Syria, 22

Tarasenko, 10, 112n27
Team B, 69
Thatcher, Margaret, 74, 86
"Theses of a Soviet Intelligence
Doctrine for the 1970s"
(Andropov), 44–45
Third World: national liberation
movements in, 57, 123n2; US
intervention in, 64
Tonkin Gulf Resolution, xviii
"Toward a Strategy of Peace"
(Kennedy), 35–36
trade war, 94
"triangular diplomacy" (US, USSR,
and China), 44
Truman, Harry, 8
Truman Doctrine, xvii, 8, 112n27
TSR (Central Intelligence Service),
125n21
Turkey, 2–3, 8, 22, 34

U-2 reconnaissance plane shootdown
over USSR in 1960, 25
Ukraine, 8
United Kingdom: seen as main
adversary by Soviet leaders prior
to World War II, xi; Soviet
infiltration of intelligence service
of, 4–6, 108n5; Soviet replacement
of ambassador to, 1; in Suez Crisis,
21–22; after World War II, xii,
xiii, xv, 1–6. *See also* Churchill,
Winston; Thatcher, Margaret
United Nations, creation of, 2
United States: after World War II,
xii–xv, 1–3; Chinese relations

United States (*continued*)
with, improvement of, 58;
Chinese-Soviet relations and, 43;
collaboration by, in World War
II, 1; Communist Party of, 41, 48;
in Crimea, 127n2; deterioration
in Soviet relations with, 57–58;
in Gulf War, 88–89, 130n37;
Hiroshima bombing by, xiv–xv;
improvement of relations with,
70–72; Iran and, 15; Khrushchev's
visit to, 24–25; in Lebanon, 22–23;
military exercises by, and Soviet
military warning system, 61,
67–70, 125n16, 126n28; nuclear
stockpile of, 7–8; Russia and,
100–101; Soviet fears of war plans
of, 6–8, 62, 110n16, 125n19, 129n20;
Soviet intelligence infiltration in,
5–6, 15–16; Soviet view of, ix, 9,
55–56, 99; Star Wars program of,
64–66; stereotypes about, 56; Third
World assistance by, 64; Vietnam
War and, xviii, 39, 42, 44
USA and Canada Institute, 41, 45
"US Foreign Policy in the Postwar
Period" (Novikov), 9, 111n23
Ustinov, Dmitry, 37, 52, 59, 61–62

Vance, Cyrus, 53
Victory (Schweizer), 94
Vienna, 2, 69
Vienna summit, 28, 58
Vietnam, 26
Vietnam War, xviii, 39, 42, 44
Voronov, Gennady, 52

Voroshilov, Kliment, 16, 52
VRYaN (Surprise Nuclear-Missile
Attack), 28, 44, 62–63, 67–69, 72,
79, 81, 83, 117n26
Vyshinsky, Andrei, 3, 13–14

Walker, John, 125n16
warning systems, military, 67–70.
See also Surprise Nuclear-Missile
Attack (VRYaN)
Warsaw Pact, xvii, 31, 32, 50, 51–52, 79
Weisband, William, 114n35
Welles, Sumner, 3
West Berlin, xvii, 2, 11–12, 23, 29–30,
116n14
West Germany, 11–12, 23, 50–51,
124n10
White House Years (Kissinger), 58–59
World War II: Soviet intelligence in,
4–8, 12–13; US, USSR, and Great
Britain collaboration in and after,
xii–xv, 1–3

Yakovlev, Aleksandr, 131n53
Yakushkin, Dmitry, 45–46
Yalta Accord, 2, 69
Yalta Conference, xvii, 2, 10, 106
Yazov, Dmitry, 65
Yeltsin, Boris, 88
Yesin, Ivan, 68

Zagladin, Vadim, 78
Zarubin, Vasily, 4
Zhdanov, Andrei, 11
Zhukhov, Georgy, 20–21, 22, 116n13
Zorin, Valerian, 14